THE WORKS
KEY STAGE 2

Every kind of poem you
will ever need for the
Literacy Hour

Chosen by Pie Corbett

MACMILLAN CHILDREN'S BOOKS

This book is dedicated to Melanie – 'only heart'

First published 2006 by Macmillan Children's Books
a division of Macmillan Publishers Limited
20 New Wharf Road, London N1 9RR
Basingstoke and Oxford
Associated companies throughout the world
www.panmacmillan.com

ISBN 978-0-330-43949-7

A CIP catalogue record for this book is available from the British Library.

Typeset by Intype Libra Ltd
Printed and bound in Great Britain
CPI Mackays, Chatham ME5 8TD

Contents

Contents

Ladles and Jellyspoons

Contents

Contents

Go Inside

Contents

Not Only

Contents

Walk Good Through the Year

Contents

Open the Door

Contents

Much Promise

Contents

Contents

Contents

Key Stage 2 – Introduction

The last six years have seen an explosion in the publishing of children's poetry. This anthology complements the range of collections that Macmillan has published recently – there are single collections by some of our finest writers (Charles Causley, Gareth Owen, Peter Dixon, Brian Moses); there are collections of quick-fire fun reads with titles such as 'The Secret Lives of Teachers' and 'Aliens Stole My Underpants', which have sold in their thousands and have turned many children on to the joys of poetry. There are also the meaty anthologies – the 'Read Me' and 'The Works' series.

Indeed, no teacher should ever be without sufficient poetry! One of the effects of so much publishing has been that many new writers have had a chance to see their work in print. This encouragement has grown a large bank of poets who work in schools, building a creative community of writers, children and teachers.

In this anthology, I have put together the essential toolkit of poems that I would want to take into any Key Stage 2 classroom. There are tried and tested favourites which have stood the test of time – and new poems that beg to be shared. Each poem has earned its place – for memorable performance as well as careful and reflective reading; as imaginative springboards to the children's own creative writing. Good poems are gifts that liberate the mind and enrich the soul. They are food for the human spirit, speaking across time and space, binding us together as many voices in one world.

I began by sorting poems out by year group and was

initially tempted to organize the anthology in this way. However, in the end I decided against that because it might limit a teacher's choice. Good poems speak to any age. Often I have found that children respond to a memorable poem even if they do not fully understand its meaning – the music and language carry their own power. Over time, a good poem pays revisiting, yielding up layers of meaning like an onion skin peeled away.

Each poem has had to earn its place – you will find the quick-fire 'single' elsewhere. This is the 'Long Player', complete with symphonies and sonatas. I sought out poems that jolt the senses, that made me feel alive, that echoed in the mind – poems that through the mediation of a good teacher would challenge and reward the reader.

Kafka said that, 'one should only read books which bite and sting . . . If the book we are reading does not wake us up with a blow to the head, what's the point in reading? A book must be the axe which smashes the frozen sea within us.' So, each poem here has that extra bite – to surprise, to challenge, to delight, to create wonder as well as the inexplicable charm of rhythmic and memorable language. There are poems that preserve and celebrate experience, both real and imagined; poems that ring true; poems that help explain the world to ourselves and, through reading, help us find our own place in the world; poems that will act as deep grooves in the memory; poems that will act as lights in the darkness; poems that touch our common genius.

Pie Corbett

They Have Places to Go

An Animal Alphabet

Alligator, beetle, porcupine, whale,
Bobolink, panther, dragon-fly, snail,
Crocodile, monkey, buffalo, hare,
Dromedary, leopard, mud-turtle, bear,
Elephant, badger, pelican, ox,
Flying-fish, reindeer, anaconda, fox,
Guinea-pig, dolphin, antelope, goose,
Humming-bird, weasel, pickerel, moose,
Ibex, rhinoceros, owl, kangaroo,
Jackal, opossum, toad, cockatoo,
Kingfisher, peacock, anteater, bat,
Lizard, ichneumon, honey-bee, rat,
Mocking-bird, camel, grasshopper, mouse,
Nightingale, spider, cuttle-fish, grouse,
Ocelot, pheasant, wolverine, auk,
Periwinkle, ermine, katydid, hawk,
Quail, hippopotamus, armadillo, moth,
Rattlesnake, lion, woodpecker, sloth,
Salamander, goldfinch, angleworm, dog,
Tiger, flamingo, scorpion, frog,
Unicorn, ostrich, nautilus, mole,
Viper, gorilla, basilisk, sole,
Whippoorwill, beaver, centipede, fawn,
Xantho, canary, polliwog, swan,
Yellowhammer, eagle, hyena, lark,
Zebra, chameleon, butterfly, shark.

Anon.

Nature's Numbers

One old observant owl
Two tame tickled trout
Three thirsty throated thrushes
Four fine fantailed fish
Five fantastically famous frogs
Six swiftly swimming salmon
Seven sweetly singing songbirds
Eight engagingly eager eels
Nine nippy and neighbourly newts
Ten tenderly tiptoeing tortoises.

John Cotton

Gorilla . . .

has a mouth
like a watermelon inside.

Teeth like seeds
when he yawns.
Eyes

like a coal black
old pit stack
smouldering there.

Did he stare?
Did he glare?

He makes me afraid.

Strange worlds in his look.
And his coat

dark as night
with bright

equatorial

stars.

Ann Bonner

The Magnificent Bull

My bull is white like the silver fish in the river,
white like the shimmering crane bird on the river bank,
white like fresh milk!
His roar is like the thunder to the Turkish cannon on the
    steep shore.
My bull is dark like the rain cloud in the storm.
He is like summer and winter.
Half of him is dark like the storm cloud,
half of him is light like sunshine.

His back shines like the morning star.
His brow is red like the beak of the Hornbill.
His forehead is like a flag, calling the people from a distance;
He resembles the rainbow.

I will water him at the river,
With my spear I shall drive my enemies.
Let them water their herds at the well;
the river belongs to me and my bull.
Drink, my bull, from the river; I am here
to guard you with my spear.

Dinka tribe

The Tyger

Tyger! Tyger! burning bright
In the forests of the night,
What immortal hand or eye
Could frame thy fearful symmetry?

In what distant deeps or skies
Burnt the fire of thine eyes?
On what wings dare he aspire?
What the hand dare seize the fire?

And what shoulder, & what art,
Could twist the sinews of thy heart?
And when thy heart began to beat,
What dread hand? & what dread feet?

What the hammer? what the chain?
In what furnace was thy brain?
What the anvil? what dread grasp
Dare its deadly terrors clasp?

When the stars threw down their spears
And water'd heaven with their tears,
Did he smile his work to see?
Did he who made the Lamb make thee?

Tyger! Tyger! burning bright
In the forests of the night,
What immortal hand or eye
Dare frame thy fearful symmetry?

William Blake

Blake's Tyger – revisited

On hearing that tigers in captivity can gradually lose their colour, losing their camouflaging stripes and fading gradually to white.

Tiger! Tiger! Turning white
In a cage just twice your height
Six paces left, six paces right,
A long slow day, a longer night.

Tiger! Tiger! Dreaming still
Of the scent? The chase? The kill?
And now? No need. No place. No scope.
No space. No point. No hope.

Tiger! Tiger! Paces. Paces.
Once he flashed through open spaces.
His world once echoed to his roars.
Now he's quiet. He stares. He snores.

An inch of sky glimpsed through the bars.
A puddle. Concrete. Smells of cars.
He sniffs the air. He slumps. He sighs.
And stares and stares through jaundiced eyes.

Michaela Morgan

Cat Began

Cat began.
She took the howling of the wind,
She took the screeching of the owl
And made her voice.

For her coat
She took the softness of the snow,
She took the yellow of the sand,
She took the shadows of the branches of the trees.

From deep wells
She took the silences of stones,
She took the moving of the water
For her walk.

Then at night
Cat took the glittering of stars,
She took the blackness of the sky
To make her eyes.

Fire and ice
Went in the sharpness of her claws
And for their shape
she took the new moon's slender curve –

And Cat was made.

Andrew Matthews

The Cat's Muse

*And the fat
cat musing on the mat
sang*

(flat):

9

I'm a tabby flabby house cat, just a fusty ball of fur,
A never-caught-a-mouse cat with a rusty sort of purr.
But sit down on the hearth mat and watch the fire with
  me.
I'll show you some of the dark and wild cats up my family
  tree.

> Oh I'm no common-or-garden cat.
> There's something you might miss:
> the sabre teeth that I unsheath
> when I stretch and yawn like this.

Sheba was a temple cat in Tutankhamun's days.
She had a hundred priestesses and several hundred slaves.
She curled up on an altar on a bed of purple silk,
Off saucers made of beaten gold she dined on camel's milk.

> Oh I'm no common-or-garden cat.
> My pedigree tends to show.
> My tail is like a cobra
> when it lashes to and fro.

Captain Moggan was a ship's cat and he sailed the Spanish
  Main.
He went all the way around Cape Horn and made it home
  again.
His claws were sharp as cutlasses. His life was sharp and
  short.
He died in Valparaiso, leaving kittens in every port.

Oh I'm no common-or-garden cat.
Haven't you noticed my
one lop ear like a pirate's hat
that flops across my eye?

Greymalkin was a black magic cat with fur as slick as
   pitch.
She held covens in a cavern with a wild and wicked witch.
And when she went out hunting on a moonlit winter's
   night
The village folk would bar their doors and dogs dropped
   dead with fright.

Oh I'm no common-or-garden cat.
Who knows what I might do?
You'd better keep me happy
or I'll put a spell . . .

         . . . on . . .

            . . .YOU!

Philip Gross

from *Fourteen Ways of Touching the Peter*

You can push
your thumb
in the
ridge

11

between his
shoulder-blades
to please him.

Starting
at its root,
you can let
his whole
tail
flow
through your hand.

In hot
weather
you can itch
the fur
under
his chin. He
likes that.

Pressing
his head against
your cheek,
you can carry
him
in the dark,
safely.

In late Autumn
you can find
seeds
adhering
to his fur.
There are
plenty.

Dumping
hot fish
on his plate, you can
fend
him off,
pushing
and purring.

You can have
him shrimp
along you,
breathing,
whenever
you want
to compose poems.

George MacBeth

My Cat Syllable

Mine. Who lies all afternoon
on the neighbour's wall drinking
sunlight, a black rag dumped out
of bottomless space on the
back garden lawn, sprawled flat on
flower beds. Who does he really
belong to?

Darkness. Two green
lamps flare in darkness. He has
drunk the sun, now the moon is
at risk. Turning his back he
dons invisibility
like the lightest tightest glove.

Brian Morse

A Saucerful of Milk

There she goes again, her cry
drifting upstairs near midnight;
so I leave my desk to find out why.

Perhaps it's food. I squeeze
a sachet of turkey into her bowl.
I call her, on my knees.

Biscuits? No, she has enough.
Company? She walks away,
banging the cat flap in a huff.

Then she's back to cry again.
I give her milk. She drinks.
(She has a saucerful, now and then.)

I rescued a bird from her claws
last week. Feathers turn up everywhere.
She is dangerous out of doors.

She is spiteful. She is cold.
Her eyes are blank. She will not
do as she is told.

Tomorrow, near midnight, her cry
will draw me downstairs.
Then, as now, I'll wonder why.

Stephen Knight

Walking a Friend's Dog
– Devon Midnight

I just can't see,
don't know
where anything is.

15

I must *imagine* hedges,
the sky, the lane ahead.
Tonight is as black
as loudspeakers,
as peppercorns, as rain-
soaked soil, as black
as a mole's eyesight
underground.

It doesn't bother the dog.
He can see with his wet
black nose, snuffling
at hedges. He can tell
where a fox has shouldered
through, can hear
the fieldmice scratch.

Tonight is black
as lofts, as cupboards
under stairs, so dark
I'm scared . . .

me . . . a grown man
from the phosphorescent city . . .
asking '*Is it time to turn back home?
Are you still there?*'

Matt Simpson

A Dog *in the* Quarry

The day was so bright
   that even birdcages flew open.
The breasts of lawns
   heaved with joy
and the cars on the highway
   sang the great song of asphalt.
At Lobzy a dog fell in the quarry
   and howled.
Mothers pushed their prams out of the park opposite
because babies cannot sleep
   when a dog howls,
and a fat old pensioner was cursing the Municipality:
they let the dog fall in the quarry and then leave him
   there,
and this, if you please, has been going on since morning.

Towards evening even the trees
   stopped blossoming
and the water at the bottom of the quarry
   grew green with death.
But still the dog howled.
            Then along came some boys
            and made a raft out of two logs
            and two planks.
            And a man left on the bank
            a briefcase . . .
            he laid aside his briefcase
            and sailed with them.

Their way led across a green puddle
to the island where the dog waited.
It was a voyage like
    the discovery of America,
a voyage like
    the quest of Theseus.
The dog fell silent,
    the boys stood like statues
and one of them punted with a stick.
The waves shimmered nervously,
tadpoles swiftly
    flickered out of the wake,
the heavens
    stood still,
and the man stretched out his hand.

It was a hand
    reaching out across the ages,
it was a hand
    linking
    one world with another,
    life with death,
it was a hand
    joining everything together,
it caught the dog by the scruff of its neck

and then they sailed back
to the music of
an immense fanfare
of the dog's yapping . . .

> *Miroslav Holub*
> *(Czechoslovakian poem*
> *trans. George Theiner)*

Wolf

Yesterday, in Crawley, I saw a white Alsatian
And out of my childhood memories leapt Wolf
The huge white Alsatian that terrified me
Every time I walked down Priors Road
Sent by my Mum on some errand to the shop.
They say animals can smell your fear;
Wolf seemed to know I was coming
Before I even left our house.
He would lie straddled across the pavement
Like some great battleship,
Or lurk shark-like, in the dark
Passageway between the houses where he lived
Ready to rise up and challenge me
With deep-throated barks that threatened invasion.
I had witnessed his ferocity when he had
Ambushed and demolished other dogs
So I would cross the road to avoid him

19

Hoping that someone else, or a car,
Would come between us.
Or, when I got to the corner and spied him,
I would turn back to tell my Mum
That the shop was closed.

Chris Eddershaw

A Riddle

Who
Wears the smartest evening dress in England?
Checks his watch by the stars
And hurries, white-scarfed,
To the opera
In the flea-ridden hen-house

Where he will conduct the orchestra?

Who
With a Robin Hood mask over his eyes
Meets King Pheasant the Magnificent
And with silent laughter
Shakes all the gold out of his robes
Then carries him bodily home
Over his shoulder,
A swag-bag?

And who
Flinging back his Dracula cloak
And letting one fang wink in the moonlight
Lifts off his top hat
Shows us the moon through the bottom of it
Then brings out of it, in a flourish of feathers,

The gander we locked up at sunset?

Ted Hughes

Owl

Owl
Was darker
Than ebony,
Flew through the night
Eyes like amber searchlights,
Rested on a post,
Feathers wind-ruffled,
Stood stump still,
Talons ready to seize
And squeeze.

Owl
Was death
That swamped the fields,
For it flew through the dark

That tightened its knot,
That bandaged the hills
In a blindfold of fear.

Owl flew – who – who – who –

Pie Corbett

What to Call a Jackdaw

sneak thief   snatch-and-grabber   artful dodger
    Jackie Braggart
cliff-cackler   folly-squatter   relic-snatcher
    back-chatter
cheeky chappie   keep-cackler   chuckle-chook
    windbagger
cock-o'-the-castle   monk's canary   glib-gob
    bluster-budgie
silly-sexton   Jack-in-the-pulpit   hop-o'-my-tomb
    flibbertigibbet
deadman's-doorman   graveyard-gossip
    sweep's-brush   sooty-bottom
scraggle-wing   petty-crow   jolly gagman
    merry-andrew
day-bat   rookster-trickster   dusk-dove
    corvus monedula
(and out from the thicket of words hopped Jack, a bit
apologetic: 'Only me!')

Philip Gross

Pheasant

Pheasant
strutting like
a lord in a green-
sheen balaclava,
trying to attract a mate,
so he can be a
father,
flicks his
tick of
yellow
eye,

hides
pride behind a
mask, displays his
vicar's collar in this
mixed-up-matching task. He preens red pencilled
feathers, shakes shavings from his back and
points a scaly leg as though he's ready
to attack but greets her with a cry
that's like a throttled engine
that's threatening
to die.

She
turns away,
this dull brown
bird, plays hard-to-
get which brings a ruffle
to his plumage, a clockwork whirr
of wings, a launching of his body,
a tearing of his mind – divided
as his airborne tail as he
leaves her behind.

Gina Douthwaite

The War God's Horse Song

I am the Turquoise Woman's son

On top of Belted Mountain beautiful horses
slim like a weasel

My horse has a hoof like striped agate
his fetlock is like fine eagle plume
his legs are like quick lightning

My horse's body is like an eagle-feathered arrow

My horse has a tail like a trailing black cloud

I put flexible goods on my horse's back

The Holy Wind blows through his mane
his mane is made of rainbows

My horse's ears are made of round corn

My horse's eyes are made of stars

My horse's head is made of mixed waters
        (from the holy waters)
        (he never knows thirst)

My horse's teeth are made of white shell

The long rainbow is in his mouth for a bridle
with it I guide him

When my horse neighs
different-coloured horses follow

When my horse neighs
different-coloured sheep follow

I am wealthy from my horse

Before me peaceful
Behind me peaceful
Under me peaceful
Over me peaceful
Around me peaceful
Peaceful voice when he neighs
I am everlasting and peaceful
I stand for my horse

Anon. (Navajo)

Birth of the Foal

As May was opening the rosebuds,
elder and lilac beginning to bloom,
it was time for the mare to foal.
She'd rest herself, or hobble lazily

after the boy who sang as he led her
to pasture, wading through the meadow flowers.
They wandered back at dusk, bone-tired,
the moon perched on a blue shoulder of sky.

Then the mare lay down,
sweating and trembling, on her straw in the stable.
The drowsy, heavy-bellied cows
surrounded her, waiting, watching, shuffling.

25

Later, when even the hay slept
and the shaft of the Plough pointed south,
the foal was born. Hours the mare
spent licking the foal with its glue-blind eyes.

And the foal slept by her side,
a heap of feathers ripped from a bed.
Straw never spread as soft as this.
Milk or snow never slept like a foal.

Dawn bounced up in a bright red hat,
waved at the world and skipped away.
Up staggered the foal,
its hooves were jelly-knots of foam.

Then day sniffed with its blue nose
through the open stable window, and found them –
the foal nuzzling its mother,
velvet fumbling for her milk.

Then all the trees were talking at once,
chickens scrabbled in the yard,
like golden flowers
envy withered the last stars.

Ferenc Juhász
from the Hungarian (trans. David Wevill)

Lizards

They emerge as arms of sun
Prise the clouds apart and stroke
The waiting, weathered wall.

Heads like probing fingertips,
Out to greet the hands that woke
Them with their golden call.

Speckled pocket dinosaurs
Dart at blink-speed from their cracks,
To stretch on smiling stones.

Summer's gift, their kiss of life,
Bathes their mottled leather backs
And lubricates their bones.

Nothing tempts their tails to twitch,
Nothing turns their polished eyes
Or troubles them, it seems.

Danger breathes her whispered call.
Stealthy wing-beats stir the skies.
They disappear like dreams.

Darren Stanley

Rat It Up

C'mon everybody
Slap some grease on those paws
Get some yellow on your teeth
And, uh, sharpen up your claws

There's a whole lot of sausage
We're gonna swallow down
We're gonna jump out the sewers
And rock this town

    Cos we're ratting it up
    Yes we're ratting it up
    Well we're ratting it up
    For a ratting good time tonight

Ain't got no compass
You don't need no map
Just follow your snout
Hey, watch out for that trap!

You can take out a poodle
You can beat up a cat
But if you can't lick a ferret
You ain't no kind of rat

    Cos we're ratting it up
    Yes we're ratting it up
    Well we're ratting it up
    For a ratting good time tonight

Now you can sneak in the henhouse
Roll out the eggs
But if the farmer comes running
Bite his hairy legs

Check the cheese for poison
Before you eat
Or you'll wind up being served up
As ratburger meat

 Cos we're ratting it up
 Yes we're ratting it up
 Well we're ratting it up
 For a ratting good time tonight

This rat was born to rock
This rat was born to roll
I don't give a monkey's
'Bout your pest control

So push off pussy-cat
Push off pup
We're the Rockin' Rodents
And we're ratting it up

 Cos we're ratting it up
 Yes we're ratting it up
 Well we're ratting it up
 For a ratting good time tonight!

Adrian Mitchell

29

Rat Race

Rat Race?
Don't make us laugh.
It's you humans
who're always in a haste.

Ever seen a rat
in a bowler hat
rushing to catch a train?

Ever seen a rat
with a briefcase
hurrying through the rain?

And isn't it a fact
that all that hurry-hurry
gives you humans heart attacks?

No, my friend,
we rats relax.

Pass the cheese,
please.

John Agard

Butterfly

This morning I found a butterfly
Against my bedroom wall.

I wanted to hold it,
To remember its colours.

But instead I guided its whirring shape
Towards the open window.

I watched it drift into the warm air,
Swaying and looping across the summer garden.

In my book I found:
'Tortoiseshell, reddish orange with yellow patches.'

But I remember its leaving,
And the pattern of its moving.

June Crebbin

The Grasshopper Glass Experiment

Above the doorway,
            a glance of green,
a place, opaque,
            on the wallpaper:
grasshopper.

31

Heat belches in from the garden, prostrates
                    the hydrangeas,
even children are mazed by the unfelt sun

and this stranger arrives in the cooler kitchen,
sprung against the ceiling, numbed and immobile.

We expect it to unfold its moon-buggy legs and
      leap,
    sailing in free-fall across the freezer
through the cirrostratus of kettle steam;

we foresee
its bright green demise,
slicked on the salad dressing,
skiing through an emergency of detergent.

Apply *Technique for the Removal of Spiders*

Apparatus: a drinking glass, dry

Method: carefully place glass over grasshopper
               ensuring legs and prawn-antennae are not
                  trapped.
               Take a slip of morning's junk mail
               and slide it 'twixt ceiling and insect.

Result: Grasshopper unwilling to relinquish cool
                      place.
                            Wait.

                      Grasshopper

                              crawls slowly

                                        in.

We examine our captive, peering
at its leaping apparatus, hoping
we have not damaged
                its spring

                            and free it in the shady dahlias.

                                        Judith Green

The Locust

What is a locust?
Its head, a grain of corn; its neck, the hinge of a knife;
Its horns, a bit of thread; its chest is smooth and burnished;
Its body is like a knife-handle;
Its hock, a saw; its spittle, ink;
Its underwings, clothing for the dead.
On the ground – it is laying eggs;
In flight – it is like the clouds.

Approaching the ground, it is rain glittering in the sun;
Lighting on a plant, it becomes a pair of scissors;
Walking, it becomes a razor;
Desolation walks with it.

> *Trad. Madagascan poem (trans.
> A. Marre and Willard R. Trask)*

A Stick Insect

A stick insect
is not a thick insect,
a macho built-like-a-brick insect,
a brawl-and-break-it-up-quick insect,
not a sleek-and-slippery-slick insect
or a hold-out-your-hand-for-a-lick insect.

No way could you say it's a cuddly pet
or a butterfly that hasn't happened yet.

And it won't come running when you call
or chase about after a ball.
And you can't take it out for a walk
or try to teach it how to talk.

It's a hey-come-and-look-at-this-quick insect,
a how-can-you-tell-if-it's-sick insect,
a don't-mistake-me-for-a-stick insect . . .

Brian Moses

34

May-Bugs

We could hear them on Summer nights
Clatter against the wire fences of the tennis courts.
Kevin, who did not mind handling those
Huge grey-brown bugs, would
Smuggle them in matchboxes
Into the chaos of our French lessons
And release them,
Secretly,
At intervals.
Great lumbering jumbo bugs
Would blunder at head height
Across the classroom of
Ducking children, flying books
And Mr Johnson
Whose anger was spectacular.

Chris Eddershaw

Porch Light

At night
the porch light
catches moths
and holds them,
trapped
and
flapping,
in a tight
yellow fist.
Only when I
turn the switch
will it loosen
its hot
grip.

Deborah Chandra

Message for the Mosquito Who Shares My Bedroom

I'm fed up
with the way
you keep me awake.

You wait
till I've just turned the light off
and settled down
for a good night's zizzzzzz
before starting up
your irritating whine.
Announcing,
'Mister Mosquito
is out for a bite.'
At any second
I expect to feel you
puncture my skin
and suck my blood.
Tiny vampire,
I'm not your personal
ketchup bottle.
If I find you've settled nearby,
I'll swat you flat.
Be warned –
go pester
some other sauce
of blood.

Pie Corbett

Icy Morning Haikus

On a frozen pond
a small dog is nervously
attempting to skate

Way up in the tree
a black cat grins with delight
watching and waiting

Beneath the clear ice
a big fish wonders if all
dogs walk on water

James Carter

Birdfoot's Grampa

The old man
must have stopped our car
two dozen times to climb out
and gather into his hands
the small toads blinded
by our light and leaping,
live drops of rain.

The rain was falling,
a mist about his white hair
and I kept saying
you can't save them all,
accept it, get back in
we've got places to go.

But, leathery hands full
of wet brown life,
knee deep in the summer
roadside grass,
he just smiled and said
they have places to go, too.

Joseph Bruchac

Hopping Frog

Hopping frog, hop here and be seen,
I'll not pelt you with stick or stone:
Your cap is laced and your coat is green;
Goodbye, we'll let each other alone.

Christina Rossetti

Black Dot

a black dot
a jelly tot

a scum-nail
a jiggle-tail

a cool kicker
a sitting slicker

a panting puffer
a fly-snuffer

a high hopper
a belly-flopper

a catalogue
   to make me
      frog

Libby Houston

Snout Doing

Said Hedgehog to Badger,
'Oh, let's marry, do –
we'll shickle and pruffle and sup hogger stew,
we'll insect each other with lice evermore,
have badgehogs in batches
and hedgers galore.
We'll live till we snuffit
twogether as one.'

Said Badger to Hedgehog,
'Oh, fleas run along.
I do get your point but I'm sett in my ways
and throughly sick of rollmantic displays
so don't take a fence, Hedge,
but this is my plot –
just go hog a headlight
and badger me not.'

Gina Douthwaite

Rabbit and Dragon

Not a fair comparison, really:
dragons don't live in hutches.
They do have shining scales,
great eyelids, burning breath.
They don't eat mash and meal
at thirty pence a pound
from the pet shop.

They sleep
long ages on their beds of gold.
People make songs about them

But rabbits don't eat children.
And nobody hunts them with bright spears.

I'd rather be a dragon
but rabbit's easier.

Tony Charles

They're Out There

The ghosts of old dragons
Drift over this town,
Their wings grown as thin
As a princess's gown,
Their scaly skin leaf-like
And wintery-brown.

The ghosts of old dragons
Are flitting round town.
Their names are lost treasures,
Each glittering noun
Thrown deep in time's ocean
Where memories drown.

The ghosts of old dragons
Keep haunting this town,
Though long-gone like gas-lamp,
Top-hat and half-crown;
Their presence as false
As the face of a clown.

The ghosts of old dragons
Go growling through town,
As upright as tombstones
Engraved with a frown;
With gravel-path voices
Which wind travels down.

Nick Toczek

The Magical Mouse

I am the magical mouse
I don't eat cheese
I eat sunsets
And the tops of trees

I don't wear fur

I wear funnels
Of lost ships and the weather
That's under dead leaves
I am the magical mouse

43

I don't fear cats

Or woodsowls
I do as I please
Always
I don't eat crusts
I am the magical mouse
I eat
Little birds – and maidens

That taste like dust

Kenneth Patchen

Jabberwocky

'Twas brillig, and the slithy toves
  Did gyre and gimble in the wabe;
All mimsy were the borogoves,
  And the mome raths outgrabe.

'Beware the Jabberwock, my son!
  The jaws that bite, the claws that catch!
Beware the Jubjub bird, and shun
  The frumious Bandersnatch!'

He took his vorpal sword in hand:
    Long time the manxome foe he sought –
So rested he by the Tumtum tree,
    And stood awhile in thought.

And, as in uffish thought he stood,
    The Jabberwock, with eyes of flame,
Came whiffling through the tulgey wood,
    And burbled as it came!

One, two! One, two! And through and through
    The vorpal blade went snicker-snack!
He left it dead, and with its head
    He went galumphing back.

'And has thou slain the Jabberwock?
    Come to my arms, my beamish boy!
O frabjous day! Callooh! Callay!'
    He chortled in his joy.

'Twas brillig, and the slithy toves
    Did gyre and gimble in the wabe:
All mimsy were the borogoves,
    And the mome raths outgrabe.

Lewis Carroll

Ladles and Jellyspoons

Ladles and Jellyspoons

Ladles and jellyspoons:
I come before you
To stand behind you
And tell you something
I know nothing about.

Next Thursday,
The day after Friday,
There'll be a ladies' meeting
For men only.

Wear your best clothes
If you haven't any,
And if you can come
Please stay home.

Admission is free,
You can pay at the door.
We'll give you a seat
So you can sit on the floor.

It makes no difference
Where you sit;
The kid in the gallery
Is sure to spit.

Trad. English

49

Tangle Talk

One dark day,
In the middle of the night,
Two dead boys
Got up to fight;
Back to back
They faced each other,
Drew their swords
And shot the other.
A deaf policeman
Heard the noise.
He stood up
And shot those boys.
If you doubt
My story's true –
Ask the blind man,
He saw it too!

*

It was midnight on the ocean
Not a streetcar was in sight.
I walked into a drugstore
To try to get a light.
The man behind the counter
Was a woman, old and grey,
Who used to peddle shoestrings
On the road to Mandalay.
The sun was shining brightly

For it rained all day that night.
It was a summer's day in winter
And the snow was raining fast,
As a barefoot boy with shoes on
Stood sitting on the grass.

Trad.

Mister Butcher-Bird

Please,
Mr Butcher-bird,
What have you got
Today?
Can I have some roast beef?
What is that
You say?
Only got a caterpillar!
Not a mutton-chop?
No,
Mr Butcher-bird,
I'll have to change
My shop!

The Perfesser and Alter Ego

51

What's Your Name?

What's your name?
Johnny Maclean.
Where do you live?
Down the lane.
What's your shop?
Lollypop.
What's your number?
Cucumber.

What's your name?
Mary Jane.
Where do you live?
Cabbage Lane.
What's your number?
Rain and thunder.
What address?
Watercress.

Trad.

Lullaby

Hush, little baby, don't say a word,
Papa's going to buy you a mocking bird.

And if that mocking bird don't sing,
Papa's going to buy you a diamond ring.

And if the diamond ring turns to brass,
Papa's going to buy you a looking glass.

And if that looking glass gets broke,
Papa's going to buy you a Billy-goat.

And if that Billy-goat runs away,
Papa's going to buy you another today.

Trad.

Alien Lullaby

Hush, little alien, don't you cry!
Mamma's gonna bake you a moonbeam pie.

And if that moonbeam pie goes stale,
Mamma's gonna catch you a comet's tail.

And if that comet's tail won't flip,
Mamma's gonna make you a rocket ship.

And if that rocket ship won't stay,
Mamma's gonna buy you the Milky Way.

And if the Milky Way's too far,
Mamma's gonna bring you a shooting star.

And if that shooting star falls down –
You're still the sweetest little alien in town!

Sue Cowling

I Ask You!

Does a catalogue ever have kittens?
Or do foxgloves ever grow mittens?
Does a cowslip ever moo?

Can a dog-rose jump up and bark?
Or a cricket bat fly after dark?
Ever seen a football in a shoe?

I ask you!

When do pussy willows ever start purring?
Or a buttercup ever need stirring?
Does a dandelion live in a zoo?

Will a moonstone ever start shining?
Or a dinosaur ever stop dining?
Ever heard a catkin saying 'Mew'?

I ask you!

Does a kitchen sink ever float?
Can you toot the horns of a goat?
Does a hare ever have shampoo?

Does a crow-bar need a big nest?
Must a sunflower set in the west?
Do sweet peas go in a stew?

I ask you!

Must a bluebottle have a cork?
Can a rambling rose get up and walk?
Does a lyre ever play true?

Have you heard a monkey-nut chattering?
Or a reindeer pitter-pattering?
Can a weathercock say 'Doodle Doo'?

I've never heard of such things.

I ask you – Have you?

David Whitehead

I saw a peacock

I saw a peacock with a fiery tail
I saw a blazing comet pour down hail
I saw a cloud all wrapt with ivy round
I saw a lofty oak creep on the ground
I saw a beetle swallow up a whale
I saw a foaming sea brimful of ale
I saw a pewter cup sixteen feet deep
I saw a well full of men's tears that weep
I saw wet eyes in flames of living fire
I saw a house as high as the moon and higher
I saw a glorious sun at deep midnight
I saw a man who saw this wondrous sight.
I saw a pack of cards gnawing a bone
I saw a dog seated on England's throne
I saw King George shut up within a box
I saw the orange driving a fat ox
I saw a butcher not a twelve-month old
I saw a greatcoat all of solid gold
I saw two buttons telling of their dreams
I saw my friends who wish I'd quit these themes.

Anon.

A Fistful of Pacifists

A thimbleful of giants
A rugby scrum of nuns
An atom of elephants
A cuddle of guns

A rustle of rhinoceros
A barrel of bears
A swear box of politicians
A bald patch of hairs

A stumble of ballet dancers
A flutter of whales
A mouthful of silence
A whisper of gales

A pocketful of earthquakes
A conference of pears
A fistful of pacifists
A round-up of squares

David Kitchen

Silly Shifts

All traffic jams jump questions.
No one can lose a dog in a hurry.
Therefore every day has a shape.

All fires have a starting point.
There is only one sky.
Therefore clouds surrender at will.

All squares have four corners.
Fish rarely swim in circles.
Therefore the ocean may look flat.

Katherine Gallagher

Talking Time

Not only the day but also the night
I am the coming and going of light

The growing and turning of shadows on land
the falling of sand, that watch on your hand

The arc of the moon, the tug of the tides
the till of the fields, the sun as it hides

The here and the now and the way back when
In hide & seek games: the counting to ten

Your birthday, your diary, your lines on your face
the start and the finish of every race

Measure me, treasure me, do as you will
I'll drag or I'll fly but I'll never stay still

If I am your rhythm, then you are my rhyme
we live for each other, and my name is time

James Carter

Short Riddles

Golden coin in blue
*

Many teeth – no bite.
*

One that holds a thousand.
*

What goes up and never comes down?
*

What has an eye but cannot see?
*

Starts on four,
Then on two,
Next on three . . .
The more it walks –
The weaker it be.
*

Around the jagged rocks
The ragged rascal ran . . .
On every bush he brushed
He left a ragged fan.

Trad.

Old English Riddle

A moth, I thought, munching a word.
How marvellously weird! a worm
Digesting a man's sayings –
A sneakthief nibbling in the shadows
At the shape of a poet's thunderous phrases –
How unutterably strange!
And the pilfering parasite none the wiser
For the words he has swallowed.

from The Exeter Book
(trans. Gerard Benson)

Goodnight

The click of a switch.

In his glass bowl the gold snake

is at once asleep.

Pamela Gillilan

Goodnight

I said my pyjamas,
I slipped on my prayers.
I went up my slippers,
I took off my stairs.
I turned off the bed,
I jumped in the light.
The reason for this . . .
You gave me a fright!

Trad.

Jack's Nature Study

That bird again. He cocked his beak: Well? Did you find them?

'Who?' I said.

Why, everybody. Everybody's somewhere. If you know where to look.

I was getting angry. What is this? Some kind of riddle?'

'Ah riddles!' He hopped a few times. 'I was hoping we'd get on to riddles. Try this for a start. It's a common-or-garden word . . .'

Each of us a day –
　　long wink
　　　　back at the sun.
We fold ourselves away,
　　we blush and shrink
　　　　when he is gone.
He loves us, loves us not,
　　we say . . .

That's our disguise.
　　We keep our mission dark,
　　　　transmitters tuned
east every morning; spies
　　in every garden, every park;
　　　　a network underground.
We have grass-roots support.
　　Day's eyes.

Philip Gross

How Did He Escape?

There was a man
in prison who was
famous for escaping –
left all his captors gaping.

So they built him a room
like a Mummy's tomb
in their finest gaol
and left him there to rot –
not a jot of a chance
to escape –
no windows,
and the doors held fast
with the largest lock
they had in stock!

All he had inside the room
was a wooden table –
and yet,
according to the fable,
ten minutes later
he was free –

So, tell me, tell me,
Alligator –
how was it done?

Pie Corbett

The Tale of the Cleverest Son

Once, not twice,
but once, there lived
an elderly man
with sons – one, two, three.
Knowing
he would soon be dead,
he called them to his bed
and said,

'I have decided
that when I die
the cleverest of three
should receive all that I have
in this world . . .'
And on to the table he hurled
three coins.
'Take one each
and go into town.
Buy what you like.
The one
who can fill
this room with the most
will inherit all that I own.'

With a groan,
the oldest filled
a wagon with bales of straw.

The second son killed
a farmyard of turkeys,
filled sack after sack
with feathers.
But the third,
slipped into a shop
and bought two
small packets
that he tucked out of sight.

That night
the father called his sons
to show how wisely
they had spent.

The oldest lad
emptied the wagon
but the straw only
covered the floor.
The second son
dragged up the sacks
and feathers flew
in all directions
but they too settled back,
barely covering the carpet.

Then the youngest son
took out two small packets
and a moment later
he had filled the room . . .

now my question to you
is simply this –
what was it
that so easily flooded
the room . . .?

Pie Corbett

Riddling Song

My love gave me a chicken, but it had no bone.
My love gave me a cherry, but it had no stone.
My love gave me a scare, without a single shiver.
My love showed me a bridge without a running river.

How can there be a chicken, without a bone?
How can there be a cherry, without a stone?
How can there be a scare, without a single shiver?
How can there be a bridge, without a running river?

When the chicken is in the egg, there is no bone.
When the cherry is in the blossom, there is no stone.
When the scare is in the field, to frighten off the crows.
When the bridge is on the face and runs across the nose.

Trad.

Galactic Punctuation

asterisk

a star
astir

a stop
astride

a
space

a spot
as steep

as
space

*

Alexis Lykiard

Maze

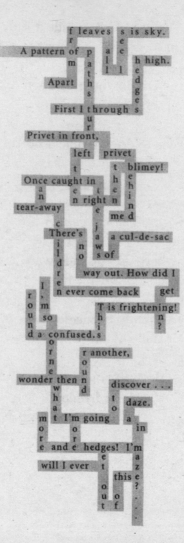

A pattern of paths of leaves is sky.
hedges high.
Apart
First I through hedges
Privet in front,
left privet blimey!
Once caught in the turn right then behind me
tear-away
There's no way of jaws of a cul-de-sac
way out. How did I ever come back get
I'm so confused. This is frightening! in?
round a corner
wonder then what round another, discover . . .
I'm going in a daze.
more and more and more hedges! I'm
will I ever get out of this maze?

Gina Douthwaite

Where?

Where do you hide a leaf?
in, if possib*l*e, *a* *f*orest.

where do you hide a wind?
among a stra*w* *in* *d*ust

where do you hide a horse?
within a clot*h* *or* *se*a.

where do you hide the sun?
behind cloud*s*, *un*der horizons.

where do you hide water?
belo*w* *a* *ter*rible flood

where do you hide a storm?
inside a gho*st* *or* *m*agician.

where do you hide a word?

Dave Calder

Sought It Out!

The rider pulled on the rain
(and got soaking wet for his trouble).

He rowed to the key.
(it opened but he could not land).

He tried to sew a pattern
(but nothing grew in the field).

He combed his hare
(but it struggled to escape).

He followed its cent
(and had enough to pay for pair).

He cooked fresh bread with flower
(and ate a primrose loaf).

He sheltered beneath an old ewe
(but its bleating woke him).

He watched the night put on his spurs
(they gleamed like stars).

He climbed the Queen's stare to bed
(and slept in her eyes).

He was pleased to reach the end of the tail
(to his surprise, it wagged happily).

Pie Corbett

Spelling Riddles

A vocal ruby
Is your glowing wordstore.

Toes in evil
Gives you square eyes.

Dice moan –
And the rest laugh.

The plane
Is a creature of the African plains.

Ken glowed
As he knew so much.

Foes rant on
Always after twelve.

O pity slim ibis
For this cannot be done.

Pie Corbett

A Puzzle

It has always been a puzzle to me
What sailors sow when they 'plough' the sea.
Does coffee go with the 'roll' of a drum?
And what sort of waiter is said to be 'dumb'?
What was it that made the window 'blind'?
Whose picture is put in a 'frame of mind'?
When a storm is 'brewing', what does it brew?
Does the 'foot' of a mountain wear a shoe?
Can a drink be got from a 'tap' on the door?
Does the 'edge' of the water cut the shore?
How long does it take to 'hatch' a plot?
Has a 'school' of herring a tutor or not?
Who is it fixes the 'teeth' of a gale?
To a king who 'reigns', why shout 'O Hail'?
Can you fasten the door with a 'lock' of hair?
Did a 'biting' wind ever bite you and where?
Who is it paints the 'signs' of the times?
Does the moon change her 'quarters' for nickels and
    dimes?
What tunes do you 'play' on your feelings, pray?
And who is it mends the 'break' of the day?
And say – I'll admit this is quite absurd –
When you 'drop' a remark, do you break your word?

Anon.

72

The Name of the Game

Play with names
And Pat becomes tap.
Karl is a lark
And Pam is a map.

Miles is smile.
Liam is mail.
Bart is a brat.
Lina's a nail.

Stan tans.
Gary turns gray.
Norma's a Roman.
Amy makes May.

Tabitha's habitat.
Leon is lone.
Kate is teak.
Mona's a moan.

Trish is a shirt.
Kay is a yak.
But whatever you do,
Jack remains Jack.

John Foster

Things for Sale on April Fool's Day

- Elbow grease
- A bottle of dry water
- A bag of hot ice
- Rubber nails
- A box of straight hooks
- A can of striped paint
- A can of worms
- A square peg for a round hole
- A kettle of fish
- An elephant's trunk
- Polly Filler
- A stale mate
- A long weight . . .

Trad.

Long-legged Italy

Long-legged Italy
Kicked poor Sicily
Right in the middle
Of the Mediterranean Sea.
Austria was Hungary,
Took a bit of Turkey,
Dipped it in Greece,
Fried it in Japan
And ate it off China.

Trad.

Lettuce Marry

Do you carrot all for me?
My heart beets for you,
With your turnip nose
And your radish face.
You are a peach.
If we cantaloupe,
Lettuce marry.
Weed make a swell pear.

Trad.

Mississippi said . . .

Mississippi said to Missouri,
'If I put on my New Jersey
what will Delaware?'
Virginia said, 'Alaska.'

Trad.

A famous painter

A famous painter
Met his death –
Because he couldn't
Draw his breath.

Trad.

Life is butter . . .

Life is butter, life is butter;
Melancholy flower, melancholy flower.
Life is but a melon, life is but a melon,
Cauliflower, cauliflower.

Trad.

Saintly Poem

St Able houses
clever horses.

St Ale lets
the beer turn flat.

St Rain keeps
trying if it pours.

St Ark sails
With the drab cat.

St Eel wriggles
but is too hard.

St Ate munches
The whole messy place.

And St One
is alone
as a cliff's face.

Pie Corbett

The Man in the Wilderness

The Man in the Wilderness asked of me
'How many blackberries grow in the sea?'
I answered him as I thought good,
'As many red herrings grow in the wood.'

The Man in the Wilderness asked me why
His hen could swim and his pig could fly.
I answered him briskly as I thought best,
'Because they were born in a cuckoo's nest.'

The Man in the Wilderness asked me to tell
The sands in the sea and I counted them well.
Says he with a grin, 'And not one more?'
I answered him bravely, 'You go and make sure!'

Anon.

My Name Is . . .

My name is Sluggery-wuggery
My name is Worms-for-tea
My name is Swallow-the-table-leg
My name is Drink-the-sea.

My name is I-eat-saucepans
My name is I-like-snails
My name is Grand-piano-George
My name is I-ride-whales.

My name is Jump-the-chimney
My name is Bite-my-knee
My name is Jiggery-pokery
And Riddle-me-ree, and ME.

Pauline Clarke

Miss Mary Mack

Miss Mary	she asked her	He jumped so
Mack	mother	high
Mack	mother	high
Mack	mother	high
all dressed in	for fifty	he reached the
black	cents	sky
black	cents	sky
black	cents	sky
with silver	to watch the	he didn't come
buttons	elephant	down
buttons	elephant	down
buttons	elephant	down
all down her	jump the	till the fifth of Ju-
back	fence	ly
back	fence	ly
back	fence	ly

Trad. (USA)

A Tree Toad Loved a She-toad

A tree toad loved a she-toad
That lived up in a tree.
She was a three-toed tree toad,
But a two-toed tree toad was he.
The two-toed toad tried to win
The she-toad's friendly nod,
For the two-toed toad loved the ground
On which the three-toed toad trod.
But no matter how the two-toed tree toad tried,
He could not please her whim.
In her tree-toad bower,
With her three-toed power,
The she-toad vetoed him.

Anon.

You!

You!
Your head is like a hollow drum.
You!
Your eyes are like balls of flame.
You!
Your ears are like fans for blowing fire.
You!

Your nostril is like a mouse's hole.
You!
Your mouth is like a lump of mud.
You!
Your hands are like drum-sticks.
You!
Your belly is like a pot of bad water.
You!
Your legs are like wooden posts.
You!
Your backside is like a mountain-top.

Igbo

Slowly

Slowly the tide creeps up the sand,
Slowly the shadows cross the land.
Slowly the carthorse pulls his mile,
Slowly the old man mounts the stile.

Slowly the hands move round the clock,
Slowly the dew dries on the dock.
Slow is the snail – but slowest of all
the green moss spreads on the old brick wall.

James Reeves

Go Inside

from *Auguries of Innocence*

To see a World in a Grain of Sand
And a Heaven in a Wild Flower,
Hold Infinity in the palm of your hand
And Eternity in an hour.

William Blake

Stone

Go inside a stone
That would be my way.
Let somebody else become a dove
Or gnash with a tiger's tooth.
I am happy to be a stone.

From the outside the stone is a riddle:
No one knows how to answer it.
Yet within, it must be cool and quiet
Even though a cow steps on it full weight,
Even though a child throws it in a river;
The stone sinks, slow, unperturbed
To the river bottom
Where the fishes come to knock on it
And listen.

I have seen sparks fly out
When two stones are rubbed,
So perhaps it is not dark inside after all;
Perhaps there is a moon shining
From somewhere, as though behind a hill –
Just enough light to make out
The strange writings, the star charts
On the inner walls.

Charles Simic

The Unwritten

Inside this pencil
crouch words that have never been written
never been spoken
never been thought

they're hiding

they're awake in there
dark in the dark
hearing us
but they won't come out
not for love not for time not for fire

even when the dark has worn away
they'll still be there

hiding in the air
multitudes in days to come may walk through them
breathe them
be none the wiser

what script can it be
that they won't unroll
in what language
would I recognize it
would I be able to follow it
to make out the real names
of everything

maybe there aren't many
it could be that there's only one word
and it's all we need
It's here in this pencil

every pencil in the world
is like this

W. S. Merwin

Air Bubble

A bubble of air
trapped under the wallpaper – oh,
the pains they took, trying to smooth me
down and out, but no,
I slipped through their fingers, I stand proud,

a bubble of the air they might
have breathed that hour, that day,
with cut grass, lilac and wild garlic,
rooks and the voice of a child
who's an old man now, calling from the end
of the garden sixty years away.

Philip Gross

Shiver My Timbers

Says the ship-
Wrecked tree,

One half split
Clean off,

Stacked
For firewood,

The other
Leaning

Groggily,
Propped up,

While the cracked
Healed-over

88

Heart wood
Is silvery

Like the lightning
Stroke itself.

Philip Gross

Hollyhock

It said on the seed packet: **Black
Hollyhock.**
Not black, like the black of my black-and-white cat –
his black's a map on his back;
not black like a female blackbird –
she's brown;
not black like the night blue sky, nor
like Gran's cellar –
that's stripey with light from the grating
up by the pavement.
    You can see people's feet
        on the street:
    clippedy heels and pointy toes,
        scuffy boots and shiny brogues,
    trainers and flip-flops,
        sandals and lace-ups
    and babies' bare feet
        kicking in pushchairs.

Not the slow sad black of funeral cars
with pretty coffins inside and the mourners
who don't look up at the soft grey clouds.
Not windows with no light on,
not the switched-off tv,
not panthers,
but something like blackberries, it is.

Judith Green

Six Ways of Looking at a Pond

1 A pond's ripple shatters faces into misery and lines.
2 A pond reflects the memories of children playing by its
   edge.
3 Sheets and sheets of lace gently laid on top of each
   other, glistening in the sunlight.
4 A pond is a net of faces and fish being dragged behind
   a trawler.
5 A pond is a glittering pocket of beads trickling into a
   bag.
6 A pond is a swan's paradise, where she gazes into the
   darkness.

Kathryn Hoblin (10 years old)

Cat in the Window

Cat in the window,
  what do you see?

Cloud, wind, leaves,
  a bird in a tree.

The daffodils shivering
  in the February breeze,

A puddle in the road
  beginning to freeze.

Snow on the wind,
  dusk in a cloud,

Leaves in a frenzy,
  the bird's head cowed.

Winter – though the sun shines.
  Blizzard, the north wind's whine.

Brian Morse

Clouds

In the clouds I saw
an old man resting in a wooden bed,
a judge's head bowing angrily.
A resting pig snorting.
A drooping Daddy
bending over
a wishing mountain.
A sulking woman sobbing.
A dove angel perched
on a rainbow tree.
A rolling brick banging
on the solid ground,
a stretching balloon popping.
A lipstick lady
driving a kissing car.
An angry crocodile
sneezing.

Teddy Corbett (7 years old)

High Places

I love high places
– the top of the hill
where the wind races
and birds come to fill

their hearts with delight
at the blue distance
their songs must aim at.
All round, the immense

sky reaches and spins;
cloud shifts and dissolves
as it imagines
shapes for cloud puzzles,

while my heart resolves
its griefs and desires
in the perspectives
of the hill's pleasures.

Then let me climb high
to where I belong;
this hill-top, where I
am cloud, space, birdsong.

John Gohorry

This Is Just to Say

I have eaten
the plums
that were in
the icebox
and which
you were probably
saving for breakfast

Forgive me
they were delicious
so sweet
and so cold

William Carlos Williams

Dinner

I regret
to say
I have eaten
your daughter.

I understand
you loved her
but she was
conveniently passing.

Forgive me
she was
such a sweet child
much love Wolfie.

Emma Beck, Natalie Squires
and Jenna O'Connell

Peach

Touch it to your cheek and it's soft
as a velvet newborn mouse
who has to strive
to be alive.

Bite in. Runny
honey
blooms on your tongue –
as if you've bitten open
a whole hive.

Rose Rauter

Pomegranates do not Feel Pain

Fasten your face on to its flesh
and suck each bead through your teeth,

dig out the pips with a tarnished teaspoon
while you sit on top of the washing machine,

squeeze half-moons on a lemon-squeezer
(make sure you're wearing a white T-shirt)

or stab your pomegranate with a whelk pin –
pomegranates do not feel pain.

Helen Dunmore

Peppermint

Put the back of your hand
nearly to your lips
and say:
Peppermint.
Two small plosive breaths brush your skin
like a child's toothpastey kiss.

Cast back your mind
to the gardens
you played in:
peppermint
filled your sunny days
crushed by hiding feet and sleeping cats.

Sweep the leaves with your palm
smell the cool sweetness;
the anaesthetized bees
peppermint-numb
stumble.

Put the back of your hand
nearly to my lips,
I will say,
Peppermint
and two small kisses brush your skin.

Judith Green

The Sound Collector

A stranger called this morning
Dressed all in black and grey
Put every sound into a bag
And carried them away

The whistling of the kettle
The turning of the lock
The purring of the kitten
The ticking of the clock

The popping of the toaster
The crunching of the flakes
When you spread the marmalade
The scraping noise it makes

The hissing of the frying-pan
The ticking of the grill
The bubbling of the bathtub
As it starts to fill

The drumming of the raindrops
On the window pane
When you do the washing up
The gurgle of the drain

The crying of the baby
The squeaking of the chair
The swishing of the curtain
The creaking of the stair

A stranger called this morning
He didn't leave his name
Left us only silence
Life will never be the same.

Roger McGough

A poem to be spoken silently . . .

It was so silent that I heard
my thoughts rustle
like leaves in a paperbag . . .

It was so peaceful that I heard
the trees ease off
their coats of bark . . .

It was so still that I heard
the paving stones groan
as they muscled for space . . .

It was so silent that I heard
a page of this book
whisper to its neighbour,
'Look, he's peering at us again . . .'

It was so still that I felt
a raindrop grin
as it tickled the window's pane . . .

It was so calm that I sensed
a smile crack the face
of a stranger . . .

It was so quiet that I heard
the morning earth roll over
in its sleep and doze
for five minutes more . . .

Pie Corbett

Listen

Silence is when you can hear things.
Listen:
The breathing of bees,
A moth's footfall,
Or the mist easing its way
Across the field,
The light shifting at dawn
Or the stars clicking into place
At evening.

John Cotton

Body Sounds

Listen –
Can you hear the
sound of the
bones grinding,
the soft beat of my heart,
the constant flowing of my blood,
the squeak of my nails
as they scrape
around my skin,
The swell of my lungs
and rolling of my tongue swirling
around my mouth
The blood seeping
through my veins,
The sound of my heart punching
the blood away
and the
moaning of the
bones.   Asleep.
Silent.   Only
the pump pumping
of my
heart.

Katya Haine (7 years old)

The Refrigerator's Belly

Always something going on in there,
little gurglings and slurps, and we feed it
all we have: butter, eggs, cheese, cold meats,
desserts in packets, tomatoes, spring onions,
left-overs, salads, ice-cubes, milkbottles.

What an investment. Its cold mouth shuts.
There's no throat, no gullet, all goes straight down
into the ice bucket of the belly, like Jonah or Gepetto,
the slow digestion working with sighs of resignation
and the waiting, waiting, waiting,

all that frozen wisdom, the opening of the door,
the world having ticked on with its comings and goings
and constant decaying.
Put your ear to the door. You can hear the meat thinking.
You can hear the cheese muttering.

Life inside the belly. Life inside the whale.

George Szirtes

The Oldest Girl in the World

Children, I remember how I could hear
with my soft young ears
the tiny sounds of the air –
tinkles and chimes
like minuscule bells
ringing continually there;
clinks and chinks
like glasses of sparky gooseberry wine,
jolly and glinting and raised in the air.
Yes, I could hear like a bat. And how!
Can't hear a sniff of it now.

Truly, believe me, I could all the time see
every insect that crawled in a bush,
every bird that hid in a tree,
individually.
If I wanted to catch a caterpillar
to keep as a pet in a box
I had only to watch a cabbage
and there it would be
crawling bendy and green towards me.
Yes, I could see with the eyes of a cat. Miaow!
Can't see a sniff of it now.

And my sense of taste was second to none,
By God, the amount I knew with my tongue!
The shrewd taste of a walnut's brain.
The taste of a train from a bridge.
Of a kiss. Of air chewy with midge.
Of fudge from a factory two miles away
from the house where I lived.
I'd stick out my tongue
to savour these in a droplet of rain.
Yes, I could taste like the fang of a snake. Wow!
Can't taste a sniff of it now.

On the scent, what couldn't I smell
with my delicate nose, my nostrils of pearl?
I could smell the world!
Snow. Soot. Soil.
Satsumas snug in their Christmas sock.
The ink of a pen.
The stink of an elephant's skin.
The blue broth of a swimming-pool. Dive in!
The showbizzy gasp of the wind.
Yes, I could smell like a copper's dog. Bow-wow!
Can't smell a sniff of it now.

As for my sense of touch
it was too much!
The cold of a snowball
felt through the vanishing heat of a mitt.
A peach like an apple wearing a vest.
The empty dish of a bird's nest.
A hot chestnut
branding the palm at the heart of the fist.
The stab of the thorn on the rose. Long grass, its itch.
Yes, I could feel with the sensitive hand of a ghost.
   Whooo!
Can't feel a sniff of it now.

Can't see a
Can't hear a
Can't taste a
Can't smell a
Can't feel a bit of it whiff of it sniff of it.
Can't get a sniff of it now.

Carol Ann Duffy

Not Only

A Chance in France

'Stay at home,' Mum said,

But I,
took a chance
in France,
turned grey
for the day
in St Tropez,
forgot
what I did
in Madrid,
had some tussles
in Brussels
with a trio
from Rio,
lost my way
in Bombay,
nothing wrong
in Hong Kong,
felt calmer
in Palma,
and quite nice
in Nice,
yes, felt finer
in China,
took a room
in Khartoum

and a villa
in Manila,
had a 'do'
in Peru
with a llama
from Lima,
took a walk
in New York
with a man
from Milan,
lost a sneaker
in Costa Rica,
got lumbago
in Tobago,
felt a menace
in Venice,
was a bore
in Singapore,
lost an ear
in Korea,
some weight
in Kuwait,
tried my best
as a guest
in old Bucharest,
got the fleas
in Belize
and came home.

Pie Corbett

Things to Do at Sandpoint

Pick a gallon of huckleberries up on Bald Mountain for
   pies and pancakes.
Go to Schweitzer for skiing.
Jump off the Pack River Bridge and do a bellyflop.
Fish for a gigantic brook trout from a pond a mile away
   from my home.
Gape as a bullmoose runs through the school field.
Watch the Bulldogs rush a long run at Bulldog Stadium.
Go jump off the dock at Sandpoint City Beach.
Win the beauty pageant. Now I'm a Snow Queen.
Get knocked over by a jumping white-tailed deer.
Play video games at Squatty Bodies.
Watch a moose eating moss from the creek by our house
   on Sunnyside Mountain.
Trot up to Lost Lakes, Idaho, on my Shetland pony named
   Christy Christmas Renee Barnes.
Rollerskate on the refinished rink at Bonner Mall.
Drive to Sunnyside to see an eagle's nest of sticks with little
   birds inside.
Take pictures of fantastic snow sculptures.
Crash the snowboard on a ski run.
Go camping and watch an eagle flip over to attack and
   claw a bird.
Break an arm at Lincoln School and faint.
Jump my bike off the docks at Lake Pend Oreille.
Swim underwater to get it.
Watch elk drink and swim in our beautiful lakes.

Go to Klondike Mike's Frozen Yogurt and ask for samples.
Get tired as heck on a 15-mile bike-a-thon.
Go to Cavanaugh's Casuals and look at the neat
    skateboard stuff.
Have more fun in Sandpoint than anywhere else.

Fifth Grade Class, Sandpoint, Idaho

Map of India

If I stare at the country long enough
I can prise it off the paper,
lift it like a flap of skin.

Sometimes it's an Advent calendar –
each city has a window
which I leave open
a little wider each time.

India is manageable – smaller than
my hand, the Mahanadi River
thinner than my lifeline.

Moniza Alvi

Leaving the Village

Rickshaws dance in the street
the bus horn moans long and low
we squash up on the plastic seat
sacks, chickens, people close.
A cow calls for its calf
in the village, across the terai
and footprints are lost in the dark
as the milky moon skims the sky.
We awake as the traffic slows
and our bus politely rolls aside
hundreds of chillies are in the road
like painted nails, in the sun to dry.
Chillies! like blood, like lips curled
leaving their soil for England
as footsteps are taken all over the world
and memories burn my tongue.

Selina Rodrigues

Sunset

Horse chestnut leaves hang
waiting like wing-folded bats
for the day to die.

Trees on hilltops creep
like caterpillar suppers
into the sun's mouth.

Blossoms blush shyly
shamed by sly, frosty fingers
that nip at night-time.

Tarmac and tussocks
seep into shared grey slumber
through day's dulling eyes.

Clusters of glow-worms
shiver down in the valley
under the dusk's thin sheet.

Over sleeping hills
a patchwork quilt of May greens
breathes for tomorrow.

Wind prays through grasses
as silent, white choirboys sway
at Today's funeral.

Gina Douthwaite

Tanka

A letter from home
wafts in the smell of sand
in the monsoon rains –
dusk falls and I hear the peal
of temple bells in the wind . . .

Usha Kishore

The Mango Tree

Tree, most certain,
right at the boulevard's end
just before the fountain,
mango tree,
I cannot pass that way
without paying homage
to your shape.
It is midwinter.
On either side, the traffic
flows past, but you stand
compact in the morning wind
under skies now blue now grey
with a green integrity.

Taufiq Rafat

Look at the Cloud-Cat . . .

Look at the cloud-cat, lapping there on high
With lightning tongue the moon-milk from the sky!

Yogeśvara, c. AD 700–800
(trans. Debjani Chatterjee)

Moonlit Apples

At the top of the house the apples are laid in rows,
And the skylight lets the moonlight in, and those
Apples are deep-sea apples of green. There goes
A cloud on the moon in the autumn night.

A mouse in the wainscot scratches, and scratches, and then
There is no sound at the top of the house of men
Or mice; and the cloud is blown, and the moon again
Dapples the apples with deep-sea light.

They are lying in rows there, under the gloomy beams;
On the sagging floor; they gather the silver streams
Out of the moon, those moonlit apples of dreams,
And quiet is the deep stair under.

In the corridors under there is nothing but sleep,
And stiller than ever on orchard boughs they keep
Tryst with the moon, and deep is the silence, deep
On moon-washed apples of wonder.

John Drinkwater

Tanka

Last night, the full moon
hung like a papery lamp
over my quiet road.
I savoured the chilly sky –
the moon tagging my shadow.

Katherine Gallagher

Hedgehog Hiding at Harvest in Hills above Monmouth

Where you hide
            moon-striped grass ripples like tiger skin
where you hide
            the dry ditch rustles with crickets

117

where you hide
>> the electricity pylon saws and sighs
>> and the combine harvester's headlight
>> pierces the hedges

where you hide
>> in your ball of silence
>> your snorts muffled
>> your squeaks and scuffles
>> gone dumb

>> a foggy moon sails over your head,
>> the stars are nipped in the bud

where you hide
>> you hear the white-faced owl hunting
>> you count the teeth of the fox.

Helen Dunmore

Midnight

Sleep is another country
We visit in our head.
I watch my brother sleeping now –
His eyelids heavy-smooth as lead . . .
A million miles away from me
Across our bedroom, in his bed.

It feels as if there's only me,
I'm the last boy left alive,
After the end of everything –
The last one to survive.
The screech owl cries, the wild wolf howls
The whole wide world's in ache.

For I am the last and lonely one
The only one left awake.

Jan Dean

Country Darkness

Now is its time.
Quiet as a vixen,
happiest under the trees
in its own rustling,
country darkness is coming.

Country darkness is coming.
Stand on a wall
high above town in the cold
and watch it fall.
Now is its time.

Now is its time.
Ghostly Kingsway where nobody lives
rolls over and sleeps
in a blanket of leaves,
country darkness is coming.

Country darkness is coming,
it was waiting all the time,
smelling of frost and leaves
with night up its sleeves,
now is its time.

Watch it wrapping up nightclubs
in velvety sleep,
watch it stopping
the late-night shopping,
watch it pinch out partygoers'
glittering clothes,
watch it stride into town.
Country darkness is coming –
now is its time.

Helen Dunmore

City Lights

Huge round oranges of light
Ripen against the thin dark of the city sky,
Spilling their juice in warm pools
        on bare dry pavements.
Below them blink the traffic lights
        like the eyes of enormous cats
Crouching in the dark –
Crouching and breathing with the
        heavy purr of the traffic;
And winking tail lights slide and dart
        like goldfish
In the pale streams pouring from
        shop windows.

Margaret Greaves

water trough

water trough
a horse
drinking sky

ai li

121

In the crisp-packet

In the crisp-packet
a blue paper twist of salt:
the night sky, the stars.

Richard Leigh

Goodnight Stroud

The Clock Tower glowers.
Its hands fidget
towards dawn.

Dark streets yawn.
  It's late –
the streets wait –
  restless as rain.

Trains idle up sidelines;
a cyclist sidles by.

Black taxis scuttle
down back alleys.

A bright bus blunders
up the High Street.

The Belisha Beacon blinks.

Parked cars huddle,
like wet toads;
the night thinks
that the stars
are sending morse-code.

Pie Corbett

City Jungle

Rain splinters town.

Lizard cars cruise by;
their radiators grin.

Thin headlights stare –
shop doorways keep
their mouths shut.

At the roadside
hunched houses cough.

Newspapers shuffle by,
hands in their pockets.
The gutter gargles.

A motorbike snarls;
Dustbins flinch.

Streetlights bare
their yellow teeth.
The motorway's cat-black tongue
lashes across
the glistening back
of the tarmac night.

Pie Corbett

Take Two

A bruise of wind
fists the street;
a knuckle of rain
punches south.

The shutters bark
back and the moon
coughs discreetly.

The fog busies itself
up some clipped alleyway.

Night nibbles dawn.

The stars lose control.

Pie Corbett

The Storm

See lightning is flashing,
The forest is crashing,
The rain will come dashing,
    A flood will be rising anon;

The heavens are scowling,
The thunder is growling,
The loud winds are howling,
    The storm has come suddenly on!

But now the sky clears,
The bright sun appears,
Now nobody fears,
    But soon every cloud will be gone.

Sara Coleridge

Rain in the City

I had only known the splash
and the pelt and the scatter,
the gush and the gurgle of gutters
and the tumbled drums of the thunder –
until I looked downwards from an upstairs office-block
and saw the sudden flowering –
a thousand umbrellas
in a most unlikely spring.

Anne Bell

Rain in the Rhondda

Cloud like the mountains closing over.
Thunder thumps on the lid of the day.
Listen to the Law that needs no preacher,
    water   *wise*   *knows how to fall*

Chains of water, pump and piston,
clanking wheels of the hills' machine.
What's it for, this heavy labour?
    nothing   *knowing*   *knows it all*

Schoolyard, graveyard, chapel, boozer
wake up blinking from a dream of coal.
Soothe the slag hills, green-grassed over.
    water   *wise*   *knows how to fall*

Something flooded, drowned some, saved some.
A river of lives that's turned to stone,
a ten-mile street that leads to nowhere,
    nothing   *knowing*   *knows it all*

Kingfisher flash and quick trout flicker.
No work's washed the river clean.
What will we do with this fruitless beauty?
    water   *wise*   *knows how to fall*

Rhondda flowing.
  Children growing.
    nothing   *knowing*   *knows it all*

Philip Gross

126

Rain

Like a drummer's brush,

the rain hushes the surfaces of tin pouches.

Emanuel di Pasquale

The Rain's Feet

The rain is slowly ticking over, then it picks up speed.
I can hear its tiny feet running every which way.

Why is it in such a hurry? It has the whole day
in front of it. And every new footstep is a new lead.

George Szirtes

Traditional Signs of Approaching Rain

When the green woodpecker cries
'Wet! Wet! Wet!'
When the cows play football
(circle round each other
and make a noise).
When the ducks 'do squacketty'.
When the cat scratches the table-leg,

127

or sneezes, or draws her paw down over
her forehead when she's washing herself.
When a cockerel flies up on to a gate, and crows.
When a dog eats grass.
When paddocks (toads) croak
on the pool at night.
When you meet a shiny-back.
When you kill a rain-clock, or God's horse.
When the hopper in the frog-spit
(or cuckoo-spit) is facing downwards.

Trad.

Wind

I pulled a hummingbird out of the sky one day but let it
    go,
I heard a song and carried it with me on my cotton
    streamers,
I dropped it on an ocean and lifted up a wave with my
    bare hands,
I made a whole canefield tremble and bend as I ran by,
I pushed a soft cloud from here to there,
I hurried a stream along a pebbled path,
I scooped up a yard of dirt and hurled it in the air,
I lifted a straw hat and sent it flying,
I broke a limb from a guava tree,
I became a breeze, bored and tired,
 and hovered and hung and rustled and lay where I could.

Dionne Brand

A lake

A lake
Is a river curled and asleep like a snake.

Thomas Lovell Beddoes

The Tide Rises, the Tide Falls

The tide rises, the tide falls.
The twilight darkens, the curlew calls;
Along the sea-sands damp and brown
The traveller hastens to the town,
And the tide rises, the tide falls.

Darkness settles on roofs and walls,
But the sea, the sea in the darkness calls;
The little waves with soft, white hands,
Efface the footprints in the sands,
And the tide rises, the tide falls.

The morning breaks; the steeds in their stalls
Stamp and neigh, as the hostler calls;
The day returns, but nevermore
Returns the traveller to the shore,
And the tide rises, the tide falls.

Henry Wadsworth Longfellow

The Sea

The sea is a hungry dog,
Giant and grey.
He rolls on the beach all day,
With his clashing teeth and shaggy jaws
Hour upon hour he gnaws
The rumbling, tumbling stones,
And 'Bones, bones, bones, bones!'
The giant sea-dog moans,
Licking his greasy paws.

And when the night wind roars
And the moon rocks in the stormy cloud,
He bounds to his feet and snuffs and sniffs,
Shaking his wet sides over the cliffs,
And howls and hollos long and loud.

But on quiet days in May and June,
When even the grasses on the dune
Play no more their reedy tunes,
With his head between his paws
He lies on the sandy shores
So quiet, so quiet, he scarcely snores.

James Reeves

For Francesca

it's so early in the morning

the cobweb
stretched between the gateposts
is not yet broken

couples
stir in their beds
and sigh and smile
and the hard
words of the day
are not yet spoken

it's so early in the morning

the street lamps go out
one by one
the small stars disappear
and your life
has barely begun

it's so early in the morning

Helen Dunmore

Small Dawn Song

This is just to say Thank You

to the tick
    of the downstairs clock
        like a blind man's stick
            tap-tip on through the dark

to the lone
    silly blackbird who sang
        before dawn when no one
            should have been listening

to the wheeze
    and chink of the milk float
        like an old nightwatchman clinking keys
            and clearing his throat

        Six o'clock and all's well
        Six o'clock and all's well

The night's been going on
                so long
                so long
This is just to say Thank You.

                                Philip Gross

This Morning I Have Risen Early

A cairn of cloud
on the mountain peak.
A curragh of cloud
on the black-blue sea.

This morning I have risen early.

A dawn-calling gull
on the scarlet seawind.
A wounded swan
and she in the scattering mist.

This morning I have risen early.

A grazing cow
on a jacket of green field.
A brindled calf
eating the buttercup buttons.

This morning I have risen early.

A razed house
as still as salt on its own grey shadow.
A rugged castle
cold as ashes in its skin of stone.

This morning I have risen early.

A spit of rock
drying black and saffron.
A thick-lipped seal
waking us with her gruff reef-songs.

This morning I have risen early.

John Rice

Not Only

Not only the leaf shivering with delight
No,
Not only the morning grass shrugging off the weight of
    frost
No,
Not only the wings of the crane fly consumed by fire
No,
Not only the steam rising from the horse's back
No,
Not only the sound of the sunflower roaring
No,
Not only the golden spider spinning
No,
Not only the cathedral window deep inside the raindrop
No,
Not only the door opening at the back of the clouds
No,

Not only flakes of light settling like snow
No,
Not only the sky as blue and smooth as an egg
No,
Not only these things

Brian Patten

Walk Good
Through the Year

Autumn Thought

Flowers are happy in summer.
In autumn they die and are blown away.
          Dry and withered,
Their petals dance on the wind
Like little brown butterflies.

                    Langston Hughes

Fog

The fog comes
on little cat feet.
It sits looking
over harbour and city
on silent haunches
and then moves on.

          Carl Sandburg

Leaves

Who's killed the leaves?
Me, says the apple, I've killed them all.
Fat as a bomb or a cannonball
I've killed the leaves.

139

Who sees them drop?
Me, says the pear, they will leave me all bare
So all the people can point and stare.
I see them drop.

Who'll catch their blood?
Me, me, me, says the marrow, the marrow.
I'll get so rotund that they'll need a wheelbarrow.
I'll catch their blood.

Who'll make their shroud?
Me, says the swallow, there's just time enough
Before I must pack all my spools and be off.
I'll make their shroud.

Who'll dig their grave?
Me, says the river, with the power of the clouds
A brown deep grave I'll dig under my floods.
I'll dig their grave.

Who'll be their parson?
Me, says the Crow, for it is well-known
I study the bible right down to the bone.
I'll be their parson.

Who'll be chief mourner?
Me, says the wind, I will cry through the grass
The people will pale and go cold when I pass.
I'll be chief mourner.

Who'll carry the coffin?
Me, says the sunset, the whole world will weep
To see me lower it into the deep.
I'll carry the coffin.

Who'll sing a psalm?
Me, says the tractor, with my gear grinding glottle
I'll plough up the stubble and sing through my throttle.
I'll sing the psalm.

Who'll toll the bell?
Me, says the robin, my song in October
Will tell the still gardens the leaves are over.
I'll toll the bell.

Ted Hughes

Cock Robin

Who killed Cock Robin?
   I, said the Sparrow,
   With my bow and arrow,
I killed Cock Robin.

Who saw him die?
   I, said the Fly,
   With my little eye,
I saw him die.

Who caught his blood?
  I, said the Fish,
  With my little dish,
I caught his blood.

Who'll make his shroud?
  I, said the Beetle,
  With my thread and needle,
I'll make the shroud.

Who'll dig his grave?
  I, said the Owl,
  With my pick and shovel,
I'll dig his grave.

Who'll be the parson?
  I, said the Rook,
  With my little book,
I'll be the parson.

Who'll be the clerk?
  I, said the Lark,
  If it's not in the dark,
I'll be the clerk.

Who'll carry the link?
  I, said the Linnet,
  I'll fetch it in a minute,
I'll carry the link.

Who'll be chief mourner?
  I, said the Dove,
  I mourn for my love,
I'll be chief mourner.

Who'll carry the coffin?
  I, said the Kite,
  If it's not through the night,
I'll carry the coffin.

Who'll bear the pall?
  We, said the Wren,
  Both the cock and the hen,
We'll bear the pall.

Who'll sing a psalm?
  I, said the Thrush,
  As she sat on a bush,
I'll sing a psalm.

Who'll toll the bell?
  I, said the Bull,
  Because I can pull,
So Cock Robin, farewell.

All the birds of the air
  Fell a-sighing and a-sobbing,
  When they heard the bell toll
For poor Cock Robin.

Anon.

November Night

Listen . . .
With faint dry sound,
Like steps of passing ghosts,
The leaves, frost-crisped, break from the trees
And fall.

Adelaide Crapsey

Still Winter

Ambushing snowdrops,
Beheading buds,
Drowning daisies
In sudden floods,

Old Mr Winter
Won't let go,
Arthritic fingers
Dipped in snow.

Grey mist clinging
Like old news,
Badger taking
One more snooze.

Blackbird singing
In freezing rain,
Screech Owl calling;
Night again.

Cold rat feasting
On the scrap-heap,
Frosty paw-prints,
Earth half-asleep.

All things hoping
Spring comes soon,
Snuggle under
Frosty moon.

Brian Patten

Frostbringer

Look, pal, I wear my hat like this for a reason.
If I straighten it, you know what happens?
The world freezes. I mean rigid;
birds in flight suddenly solid,
falling on to smashed ponds. Tilt
this titfer and the whole earth spills
from its axis, winter sweeps in. I can
do that. Call it a gift.

                    And then
rivers set instantly, waterfalls in mid crash,
out of the taps only a drip that freezes.
Solid ice stoppers will rise from milk bottles
and kiddies will cry and everyone's heart
go hard. Beggars will be ignored
and no one give to charity, concert halls
and churches cold as graves. Brother, If I
wanted I could close down every motorway
and every airport and seal the planet
in a swirling net of white. Old men
would drop dead and foxes come to farms
and everyone be trapped in their own doors,
cities would starve and governments fall
and no one would love his neighbour at all
because my snow would be head high
and blanketing the kingdom.
                    So I
keep the jaunty angle. By such small
mercies, these few degrees, do we survive.

                                Catherine Fisher

The Frozen Man

Out at the edge of town
where black trees
crack their fingers
in the icy wind
and hedges freeze
on the shadows
and breath of cattle,
still as boulders,
hangs in rags
under the rolling moon
a man is walking
alone:

on the coal-black road
his cold
feet
ring
and
ring.
Here in a snug house
at the heart of town
the fire is burning
red and yellow and gold:
you can hear the warmth
like a sleeping cat
breathe softly
in every room.
When the frozen man

147

comes to the door,
Let him in,
let him in,
let him in.

Kit Wright

December Moon

The moon has come out too soon,
it's still the middle of the afternoon
and the day shows no sign of darkness.

What is the moon doing,
sneaking into the sky when it's light?

What is the moon playing at?
Couldn't it sleep?
Has its alarm clock rung too soon?

Do we see the moon this early
in June or September?

Or does December bring a special moon,
a let's-get-these-nights-over-soon moon,
a can't-wait-for-Christmas-to-come moon?

Brian Moses

148

Chips

Out of the paper bag
Comes the hot breath of the chips
And I shall blow on them
To stop them burning my lips.

Before I leave the counter
The woman shakes
Raindrops of vinegar on them
And salty snowflakes.

Outside, the frosty pavements
Are slippery as a slide
But the chips and I
Are warm inside.

Stanley Cook

Mid-Winter Haiku

Ice on the windows,
tangerine peeled in one curl
under the duvet

Christmas in prison,
barbed wire glitters in searchlights –
a fence made of stars.

Two plastic reindeer,
a shopping bag of holly,
a mouth of frost.

Chocolate fever –
we dig for gold-wrapped treasure
deep in our stockings.

Helen Dunmore

Christmas Eve. The mice go to Midnight Mass

In the dark flickering candlelight excitement
of nearly Christmas Day
the mice play silver shadows in their winter coats,
paw prints of stars tumbling through the straw manger.

Judith Green

Three Kings

Out of the wintry shadows wind sped like an arrow
earth and water froze.
Albert wheeled his barrow,
leaning on his load. 'Christmas Day tomorrow'.
'On the downs it snowed,' cried George, 'it's coming soon.'
Frank looked up the road.

150

That dark afternoon a stranger walked ahead
haloed by the moon.
He half turned: 'Peace,' he said.
Wind dropped.
Like a sign a star rose up,
and led that moment out of time,
as if his gentle call
made earth and heaven rhyme.

Like a miracle
George, Frank and Albert felt
drawn into his will.

Lamplight seemed to melt,
with a wild grace stars circled down
To pelt wheelbarrow and cars.

The three men hid their eyes
as love shook off its bars, and earth met paradise.

He left them in the falling snow,
with memories too strange for reckoning,
like his star that rose
and made each one a king.

Susan Skinner

The Warm and the Cold

Freezing dusk is closing
   Like a slow trap of steel
On trees and roads and hills and all
   That can no longer feel.
      But the carp is in its depth
         Like a planet in its heaven.
      And the badger in its bedding
         Like a loaf in the oven.
      And the butterfly in its mummy
         Like a viol in its case.
      And the owl in its feathers
         Like a doll in its lace.

Freezing dusk has tightened
   Like a nut screwed tight
On the starry aeroplane
   Of the soaring night.
      But the trout is in its hole
         Like a chuckle in a sleeper.
      The hare strays down the highway
         Like a root going deeper.
      The snail is dry in the outhouse
         Like a seed in a sunflower.
      The owl is pale on the gatepost
         Like a clock on its tower.

Moonlight freezes the shaggy world
  Like a mammoth of ice –
The past and the future
  Are the jaws of a steel vice.
    But the cod is in the tide-rip
      Like a key in a purse.
    The deer are on the bare-blown hill
      Like smiles on a nurse.
    The flies are behind the plaster
      Like the lost score of a jig.
    Sparrows are in the ivy-clump
      Like money in a pig.

Such a frost
  The flimsy moon
    Has lost her wits.

    A star falls.

The sweating farmers
  Turn in their sleep
    Like oxen on spits.

Ted Hughes

A Boat in the Snow

On to the ocean's cold dark skin
Snowflakes are falling and are melting away.
How strange the snow seems out here!
How quickly the white blizzard is swallowed up by the
   waves.
Without the framework of land
Each flake's transformed.
Like a trillion ocean-borne moths
They flick into existence, then go.
As the sky above and around me
Glitters with frosty flecks of stars
So the deck of the boat glitters,
And I wonder, are whales sleeping
Out there in the world's depth beyond
The boat's bow? And I wonder,
Do they really sleep? And how?
There is no one to ask.
Snuggled up in cabins
Passengers are dreaming,
And all round us still the snow is falling,
And the ship's deck has become
A moonlit field, a field adrift
On the dark skin of the world.
I would love to sail forever between islands of snow.

Brian Patten

November

No sun – no moon!
No morn – no noon –
No dawn – no dusk – no proper time of day –
    No sky – no earthly view –
    No distance looking blue –
No road – no street no 't' other side the way' –
    No end to any Row –
    No indications where the Crescents go –
    No top to any steeple –
No recognitions of familiar people –
No courtesies for showing 'em –
    No knowing 'em –
No travelling at all – no locomotion –
No inkling of the way – no notion –
    'No go' – by land or ocean –
    No mail – no post –
No news from any foreign coast –
No Park – no Ring – no afternoon gentility –
    No company – no nobility –
No warmth, no cheerfulness, no healthful ease,
    No comfortable feel in any member –
No shade, no shine, no butterflies, no bees,
    No fruits, no flowers, no leaves, no birds –
    November!

                                        Thomas Hood

December

De snow, de sleet, de lack of heat,
De wishy-washy sunlight,
De lip turn blue, de cold, 'ACHOO!'
De runny nose, de frostbite

De creakin' knee, de misery
De joint dem all rheumatic,
De icy bed (de blanket dead),
De burs' pipe in de attic

De window a-shake, de glass near break,
De wind dat cut like razor
De wonderin' why you never buy
De window from dat double-glazer

De thick new coat, zip up to de throat,
De nose an' ears all pinky,
De weepin' sky, de clothes can't dry,
De days dem long an' inky.

De icy road, de heavy load,
De las' minute Christmas shoppin'
De cuss an 'fret' cause you feget
De ribbon an' de wrappin'.

De mud, de grime, de slush, de slime,
De place gloomy since November,
De sinkin' heart, is jus' de start
O'de wintertime,
December.

Valerie Bloom

Red Boots On

Way down Geneva,
All along Vine,
Deeper than the snow drift
Love's eyes shine:

Mary Lou's walking
In the winter time.

She's got

Red boots on, she's got
Red boots on,
Kicking up the winter
Till the winter's gone.

So

Go by Ontario,
Look down Main,
If you can't find Mary Lou,

Come back again:

Sweet light burning
In winter's flame.

She's got

Snow in her eyes, got
A tingle in her toes
And new red boots on
Wherever she goes

So

All around Lake Street,
Up by St Paul,
Quicker than the white wind
Love takes all:

Mary Lou's walking
In the big snow fall.

She's got

Red boots on, she's got
Red boots on,
Kicking up the winter
Till the winter's gone.

Kit Wright

Thaw

Over the land freckled with snow half-thawed

The speculating rooks at their nests cawed

And saw from elm-tops, delicate as flower of grass,

What we below could not see. Winter pass.

Edward Thomas

Sunday Morning Diary Poem

This Sunday morning
surprised by birdsong.
Sun warms roofs,
casts cool sharp shadows –

though the road glitters.
Frost gilds
             each
                     step.

Daisy and Teddy
run on ahead,
their voices echo
up the narrow lane
to Sunday school.

A marmalade cat
sneaks by greystone walls,
a blackbird sets off an alarm,
calls an early warning . . .

Trees are still skeletal,
form stark patterns
against a blue sky.

After weeks of grey fog
and sudden snow –
it feels good
to know the sun's
kindly glow –

to catch bird song
as it drifts along
the lanes.

Pie Corbett

The Visitor

Cold fingers clawed the face of earth,
Bold winter strutted round,
Bare branches trembled in the wind,
Their leaves mulching the ground.
Dancing snowflakes chuckled in the
Prancing north-east breeze,
Algid river stood still, crippled,
Aged women coughed and wheezed.
Sheep shivered in the snow-bound wasteland,
Steep and icy were the paths.
In the houses, people huddled,
Skin slowly cooking round the hearths.
Then it happened, one clear morning,
When the bite of cold was sore,
That there came a gentle knocking
At the weatherman's cottage door.
He got up and shambled out to
See, his heart began to sing,
By the door, a young girl smiling,
'Hi,' she said. 'My name is Spring.'

Valerie Bloom

From My Diary, July 1914

Leaves
  Murmuring by myriads in the shimmering trees.
Lives
  Wakening with wonder in the Pyrenees.
Birds
  Cheerily chirping in the early day.
Bards
  Singing of summer, scything through the hay.
Bees
  Shaking the heavy dews from bloom and frond.
Boys
  Bursting the surface of the ebony pond.
Flashes
  Of swimmers carving through the sparkling cold.
Fleshes
  Gleaming with wetness to the morning gold.
A mead
  Bordered about with warbling waterbrooks.
A maid
  Laughing the love-laugh with me; proud of looks.
The heat
  Throbbing between the upland and the peak.
Her heart
  Quivering with passion to my pressed cheek.
Braiding
  Of floating flames across the mountain brow.
Brooding
  Of stillness; and a sighing of the bough.

Stirs
   Of leaflets in the gloom; soft petal-showers;
Stars
   Expanding with the starr'd nocturnal flowers.

Wilfred Owen

Springwind

Gauge the wind: peg the sheets
to billow full, a sail in the gulping breeze;
   anchor fast the flapping towels
and toe the socks tight to line.
   Underwear, emboldened
throws caution to the wind
              uninhibits bits and things,
high-propped
and strutting.
The slap and crack of washing
             jostles over spring,
exhilarating.
And blackbirds spar and tussle,
    excavate the mulched leaves of winter
black in black
    not slacking, even as the clothes
join sleeve and hem
    above them.

Judith Green

163

Heatwave

Heat over all; a lark can rise
Into the arching sun;
The moor like a lion sleeping lies –
Rough mane on burning stone.
Not a harebell shakes; the wild blue flags
Of wind are folded up.
Here on the hill the air is still
As water in a cup.

Phoebe Hesketh

To Make a Prairie

To make a prairie it takes a clover
        and one bee,
One clover, and a bee.
And revery.
The revery alone will do,
If bees are few.

Emily Dickinson

Making the Countryside

Take a roll of green,
Spread it under a blue or blue-grey sky,
Hollow out a valley, mould hills.

Let a river run through the valley,
Let fish swim in it, let dippers
Slide along its surface.

Sprinkle cows in the water-meadows,
Cover steep banks with trees,
Let foxes sleep beneath, the owls above.

Now, let the seasons turn,
Let everything follow its course.
Let it be.

June Crebbin

Summer Rain

Here it is so quiet
you can hear the twigs
whispering to each other.
Every leaf sags
under the heavy gold of the sun.
Such a wealth of gold
even the day stands still
holds its breath
to keep the gold from spilling
down into the weeds and underbrush

Georgi Djagarov

The Red Wheelbarrow

so much depends
upon

a red wheel
barrow

glazed with rain
water

beside the white
chickens

William Carlos Williams

166

The Beach

The beach is a quarter of golden fruit,
a soft ripe melon
sliced to a half-moon curve,
having a thick green rind
of jungle growth;
and the sea devours it
with its sharp white teeth.

W. Hart-Smith

Beach

Dry whisper of seagrass.
My feet and legs are bare.
Strong and steady stiff sea wind
is tearing at my hair.
Cold sun's hand across the land
bleached and pale as bone.
Sandscape, landscape lunar dunes
blown for me alone.

Ann Bonner

Goodbye Now

Walk well
Walk well
Don't let thorns run in you
Or let a cow butt you.
Don't let a dog bite you
Or hunger catch you, hear!

Don't let sun's heat turn you dry.
Don't let rain soak you.
Don't let thief rob you
Or a stone bump your foot, hear!
Walk well
Walk well

James Berry

'Bye Now

Walk good
Walk good
Noh mek macca go juk yu
Or cow go buk yu,
Noah mek dog bite yu
Or hungry go ketch yu, yah!

168

Noh mek sunhot turn you dry.
No mek rain soak yu.
Noh mek tief tief yu.
Or stone go buck yu foot, yah!
Walk good
Walk good

James Berry

Open the Door

Swing Low

Swing low, sweet chariot,
Coming for to carry me home!
Swing low, sweet chariot,
Coming for to carry me home!

I looked over Jordan and what did I see?
Coming for to carry me home!
A band of angels coming after me,
Coming for to carry me home!

If you get there before I do,
Coming for to carry me home!
Tell all my friends I'm coming too,
Coming for to carry me home!

Swing low, sweet chariot,
Coming for to carry me home!
Swing low, sweet chariot,
Coming for to carry me home!

Trad. (USA)

Mamma Dot

Born on a Sunday
in the kingdom of Ashante

Sold on a Monday
into slavery

Ran away on Tuesday
'cause she born free

Lost a foot on Wednesday
when they catch she

Worked all Thursday
till her hair grey

Dropped on a Friday
when they burned she

Freed on a Saturday
in a new century

Fred D'Aguiar

Dry Your Tears, Africa!

Dry your tears, Africa!
Your children come back to you
their hands full of presents
and their hearts full of love.
They return to clothe you
in their dreams and their hopes.

Bernard Dadié (Côte d'Ivoire)

Young Africa's Lament

I am half-starved;
I asked for bread they gave me stone.
I am thirsty;
I asked for water they gave me slush.
They tell the horse to wait awhile
Because green grasses would soon grow
And dry Sahara would yield great streams.

Dennis Chukude Osadebay

A Heart

A heart to hate you
Is as far as the moon.
A heart to love you
Is near as the door.

Trad. (Burundi)

The door

Go and open the door.
Maybe outside there's
a tree, or a wood,
a garden,
or a magic city.

Go and open the door.
Maybe a dog's rummaging.
Maybe you'll see a face,
or an eye,
or the picture
of a picture.

Go and open the door.
If there's a fog
it will clear.

Go and open the door.
Even if there's only
the darkness ticking,
even if there's only
the hollow wind,
even if
nothing
is there,
go and open the door.

At least
there'll be
a draught.

Miroslav Holub

In My Country

In my country they jail you
For what they think you think.
My uncle once said to me:
They'll implant a microchip
In our minds
To flash our thoughts and dreams
On to a screen at John Vorster Square.
I was scared:
By day I guard my tongue
By night my dreams.

Pitika Ntuli

Whose Dem Boots

Whose dem boots ah hearin, chile,
Whose dem boots ah hear?
Whose dem boots ah hearin, chile,
Whose dem boots ah hear?
Dem boots trampin down de road
Dat fill mah heart wid fear?

Gotta fin' me a hid'n place,
Whai, whai,
Gotta fin' me a hid'n place.

Whose dem boots ah hearin, chile,
Comin thru mah gate?
Whose dem boots ah hearin, chile,
Comin thru mah gate?
Trampin straight up to mah door?
Tell dem please to wait.

Gotta fin' me a hid'n place,
Whai, whai,
Gotta fin' me a hid'n place.

Whose dem boots ah seein, chile,
Stand'n by mah bed?
Whose dem boots ah seein, chile,
Stand'n by mah bed?
Waitin' dere so patient, chile?
Tell dem go ahead.

Gotta fin' me a hid'n place,
Whai, whai,
Gotta fin' me a hid'n place.

Valerie Bloom

Mango, Little Mango

The mango stands for Africa
    In its taste
    In its smell
    In its colour
    In its shape

The mango has the shape of a heart –
    Africa too!
It has a reddy-brown shade
Like the tanned plains
Of my beloved earth.
Because of this I love you and your taste
    Mango!
Heart of fruit, sweet and mild.

You are the love of Africa
Because beating in your breast
    Is Africa's heart,
    Oh mango, little mango,
    Love of Africa!

Anon.

Bells of Rhymney

O what can you give me?
Say the sad bells of Rhymney.

Is there hope for the future?
Cry the brown bells of Merthyr.

Who made the mineowner?
Say the black bells of Rhondda.

And who robbed the miner?
Cry the grim bells of Blaina.

They will plunder willy-nilly,
Say the bells of Caerphilly.

They have fangs, they have teeth!
Shout the loud bells of Neath.

To the south, things are sullen,
Say the pink bells of Brecon.

Even God is uneasy,
Say the moist bells of Swansea.

Put the vandals in court!
Cry the bells of Newport.

All would be well if – if – if –
Say the green bells of Cardiff.

Why so worried, sisters, why?
Sing the silver bells of Wye.

Idris Davies

Playground Song

I'm the one in calipers
Who makes the people stare –
I used to lie awake at night
And think it wasn't fair,
But since I've found a proper friend
I really couldn't care . . .

She told her mum
                    that I'm the one
With lovely curly hair.

Clare Bevan

Such Times

I walk across the playground. And all of a sudden
a six-year-old boy rushes to me
with wild strawberry cheeks.
In his hand he clutches a pop gun.
'Bang! Bang!' – he shoots at me.
then he sticks the weapon in his pocket.
'Gotcha!' – he says and runs off.

I notify the family. Friends.
I phone the police and report my death.
They spread their helpless hands.
'Such times' – they say.

Ewa Lipska

Sunfire

'Who'll set me alight?'
said the wood one dark night.
'I'll have some fun,'
said the wakening sun.
'I'll set you on fire
as I climb higher and higher.'

'Who'll fan the flame?'
said the branch on its frame.
'I'll blow the trees,'
said the gathering breeze.
'I'll fan the fire
for my lungs never tire.'

'Who'll run from the blaze?'
said the deer in a daze.
'I'll warn the pack,'
said the fox at the back,
'I'll raise the alarm
and we'll come to no harm.'

'Who'll douse the embers?'
said the owl who remembers.
'I'll sting the glow,'
said the rain in its flow,
'I'll kill the flame;
let me take the blame.'

'Who'll grow us again?'
said the forest in pain.
'We'll take your seed,'
said the earth, lake and reed,
'We'll start the cycle again,
for this world must not wane.'

John Rice

Extract from a letter containing two gold maple leaves, 1915

. . . this is a picture, for you,
this is all I can give
from so far away. Unframed:
a clay field
hung with damp November;
spears of wheat piercing the clods
as if the flick of an artist's brush
has spattered with green
the grey;
maple trees still braided with a few leaves
and under my feet the remains of a gold counterpane
on winter's bed;
the field's edge webbed
with tall grasses bending heavy;
the echoing rooks in the big sky;
dewdrops pearled grey and glistening on barbed wire
not far from the front line . . .

Judith Green

In Memoriam (Easter, 1915)

The flowers left thick at nightfall in the wood
This Eastertide call into mind the men,
Now far from home, who, with their sweethearts, should
Have gathered them and will do never again.

Edward Thomas

The Apple-Raid

Darkness came early, though not yet cold;
Stars were strung on the telegraph wires;
Street lamps spilled pools of liquid gold;
The breeze was spiced with garden fires.

That smell of burnt leaves, the early dark,
Can still excite me but not as it did
So long ago when we met in the park –
Myself, John Peters and David Kidd.

We moved out of town to the district where
The lucky and wealthy had their homes
With garages, gardens, and apples to spare
Ripely clustered in the trees' green domes.

We chose the place we meant to plunder
And climbed the wall and dropped down to
The secret dark. Apples crunched under
Our feet as we moved through the grass and dew.

The clusters on the lower boughs of the tree
Were easy to reach. We stored the fruit
In pockets and jerseys until all three
Boys were heavy with their tasty loot.

Safe on the other side of the wall
We moved back to town and munched as we went.
I wonder if David remembers at all
That little adventure, the apples' fresh scent.

Strange to think that he's fifty years old,
That tough little boy with scabs on his knees;
Stranger to think that John Peters lies cold
In an orchard in France beneath apple trees.

Vernon Scannell

Wings

If I had wings
    I would touch the fingertips of clouds
        and glide on the wind.

If I had wings
    I would taste a chunk of the sun
        as hot as peppered curry.

If I had wings
    I would listen to the clouds of sheep bleat
        that graze on the blue.

If I had wings
    I would breathe deep and sniff
        the scent of raindrops.

If I had wings
    I would gaze at the people
        who cling to the earth.

If I had wings
    I would dream of
        walking the deserts
            and swimming the seas.

Pie Corbett

The Oubliette

The past is brambled over, smothered.
I could have stepped
off into darkness and be lying undiscovered
down there yet.

How long had an uneasy memory
  of it slept
beneath its grille of ferns? It glistened inwardly,
  so wet

it might have been a wishing-well
  except
no wish was granted. This was the forgetting-cell,
  the oubliette.

How long did it take them, simply
  being kept
to die? Someone, somewhere, is dying now. So easy
  to forget.

Philip Gross

Coltsfoot

Coming before my birthday they are forever your flowers

Who are dead and at whose hand

I picked them on the allotments and blitzed land.

David Constantine

Yes

A smile says: Yes.
A heart says: Blood.
When the rain says: Drink
The earth says: Mud.

The kangaroo says: Trampoline.
Giraffes say: Tree.
A bus says: Us
While a car says: Me.

Lemon trees say: Lemons.
A jug says: Lemonade.
The villain says: You're wonderful.
The hero: I'm afraid.

The forest says: Hide and Seek.
The grass says: Green and Grow.
The rail says: Maybe.
The prison says: No.

The millionaire says: Take.
The beggar says: Give.
The soldier cries: Mother!
The baby sings: Live.

The river says: Come with me.
The moon says: Bless.
The stars say: Enjoy the light.
The sun says: Yes.

Adrian Mitchell

Grandmother

Rain falls on warm tin roofs
like a thousand pearls.

The air is thick with ripe mangoes,
chickens scratch in the yard,

Bibi stands on the veranda
holding me in a tight hug,
her perfume of betel nut.

On the night she died
I dreamt of her:
of carrying water
to quench her thirst.

Contributor to First Words

Life Without You

blossom bloom
blossom moss
blossom fall
blossom loss
blossom less
that is life without you
I guess.

Dan Cockrill

Goodbye (Cinquain)

And so
as evening falls
I close the curtains on
the empty bed. And shadows creep
inside.

Valerie Bloom

And My Heart Soars

The beauty of the trees,
the softness of the air,
the fragrance of the grass,
    speaks to me.

The summit of the mountain,
the thunder of the sky,
the rhythm of the sea,
    speaks to me.

The faintness of the stars,
the freshness of the morning,
the dew drop on the flowers,
    speaks to me.

The strength of the fire,
the taste of salmon,
the trail of the sun,
and the life that never goes away,
    they speak to me.

And my heart soars.

Chief Dan George

Much Promise

South to North; 1965

I was born south of the river
down in the delta, beyond the bayou
lived in the swamps just off the High Street
London alligators snapping my ankles.

It was Bromley, Beckenham, Penge, Crystal Palace
where the kids said *wotcha*, ate bits of *cike*,
the land my father walked as a boy
the land his father walked before him.

I was rooted there, stuck in the clay
until we drove north, moved to Yorkshire
a land of cobbles, coal pits and coke works,
forges and steel, fires in the sky.

Where you walked through fields around your village
didn't need three bus-rides to see a farm.

It was Mexbrough, Barnsley, Sprotbrough, Goldthorpe
I was deafened by words, my tongue struck dumb
gobsmacked by a language I couldn't speak in.

Ayop, sithee, it's semmers nowt
What's tha got in thi snap, chaze else paze?
Who does tha suppoort, Owls else Blades?
Dun't thee tha me, thee tha thi sen
Tha's a rate 'un thee, giz a spice?

Cheese and peas, sweets and football
I rolled in a richness of newfound vowels
words that dazed, dazzled and danced
out loud in my head until it all made sense
in this different country, far away
from where I was born, south of the river.

David Harmer

Old Tongue

When I was eight, I was forced south.
Not long after, when I opened
my mouth, a strange thing happened.
I lost my Scottish accent.
Words fell off my tongue:
eedyit, dreich, wabbit, crabbit,
stummer, teuchter, heidbanger,
so you are, so am ur, see you, see ma ma,
shut yer geggie, or I'll gie you the malkie!

My own vowels started to stretch like my bones
and I turned my back on Scotland.
Words disappeared in the dead of night,
new words marched in: ghastly, awful,
quite dreadful, scones said like stones.
Pokey hats into ice-cream cones.
Oh where did all my words go —
my old words, my lost words?

Did you ever feel sad when you lost a word,
did you ever try and call it back
like calling in the sea?
If I could have found my words wandering,
I swear I would have taken them in,
swallowed them whole, knocked them back.
Out in the English soil, my old words
buried themselves. It made my mother's blood boil.
I cried one day with the wrong sound in my mouth.
I wanted them back; I wanted my old accent back,
my old tongue. My dour, soor Scottish tongue.
Sing-songy. *I wanted to gie it laldie.*

Jackie Kay

Language for Sale

Language is spawned on the island
easily as fish eggs
and yet who is it that speaks?
  that is what counts!

White, Black or native speaker? . . .
and when there is no native,
the immigrants quarrel,
  Babel-like.

Language is to do with money, power
you speak it right,
    you get a job
you speak it wrong,
    it will stick in your throat
like a frog croaking
wrong notes all the time.

The leftovers of the colonists
like stale breath and fungied bread
smells bad,
to grow identity
more than your photo-cards with meaningless numbers,
you want your language
the desire grows like a child in the womb.

The long remembered, half-erased memories of
    lullabies,
of harsh nights dawning out into
terrifying days,
    coolie days
I need a language
a language which would mean what I say
which would unearth my leanings – my nuances
and not drawl dictionary meanings back at me . . .

I want my language!

Shakuntala Hawoldar

Bengali Language

We speak in Bengali
We write in Bengali
We see the entire world
Through its green glow

We adorn the minarets of our minds
With its countless flowers
Illuminating the sky

With its light in our hands
We journey across the world
Through its sweet melody
We learn the languages of others

Rabindranath Tagore
(trans. Anwara Jahan)

From Sylhet to Sheffield

My village in Sylhet has many streams.
Small and friendly, they invited our play;
each day after school I'd go with my friends,
we'd splash in the waters and sing and shout.
I thought this life would go on forever.

Then my family flew across the seas.
Everything was strange in a foreign land:
the language, the food, the weather, the school.
My world was upside down and I'd rush home
each day after school. I longed to fly back.

Sheffield was so large – I longed to escape
but its small and friendly streams spoke of home.
With my sisters and brothers I grew up
in this city, learned English and made friends.
Now our children play beside the canal.

Mina Begum

Our Street

Our street is not a posh place,

Say the mums in curlers, dads in braces,
    kids in jeans.
Our street is not a quiet place,

Says our football match, our honking bikes,
    our shouts.
Our street is not a tidy place,

Say the lolly wrappers, chippie bags, and
    written-on walls.
Our street is not a lazy place,

Say the car washing dads, clothes washing mums,
    and marbling boys.
Our street is not a short one,

Says milkman Jim, and postman Joe
    and rentman.
Our street is not a new place,

Say the paint-peeled doors, pavements worn,
    and crumbly walls.
Our street is not a green place,

Say the pavements grey, forgotten gardens,
    lines of cars.
But our street is the best

    Says me!

Les Baynton

Rupa's Hand

Can you sketch?
Rupa can.
A house, a horse, a mouse, a man.

Her hand is the pencil bird,
Watch it fly,
Looping the loop
Through the sketchbook sky.

201

Can you paint?
Rupa's the best.
A fish, a fire, a treasure chest.

Her hand is the brush dancer,
Watch it wind
Through a pencilled maze,
Leaving trails behind.

Can you draw?
Rupa's great.
A chair, a child, a garden gate.

Her hand is the pastel shark,
Watch it slash
Through coloured seas
With a rainbow splash.

Can you shade?
Rupa does.
A smudge, a smear, a feathered fuzz.

Her hand is the charcoal flower,
Watch it grow,
Shedding fine, grey seeds
On white fields below.

Can you hear
Rupa's heart?
Its beat is captured in her art.

Darren Stanley

A boy's head

In it there is a space-ship
and a project
for doing away with piano lessons.

And there is
Noah's ark,
which shall be first.

And there is
an entirely new bird,
an entirely new hare,
an entirely new bumble-bee.

There is a river
that flows upwards.

There is a multiplication table.

There is anti-matter.

And it just cannot be trimmed.

I believe
that only what cannot be trimmed
is a head.

There is much promise
in the circumstance
that so many people have heads.

Miroslav Holub
(trans. Ian Milner)

A Girl's Head
(after the poem, 'A Boy's Head' by Miroslav Holub)

In it there is a dream
that was started
before she was born,

and there is a globe
with hemispheres
which shall be happy.

There is her own spacecraft,
a chosen dress
and pictures of her friends.

There are shining rings
and a maze of mirrors.

There is a diary
for surprise occasions.

There is a horse springing hooves
across the sky.

There is a sea that
tides and swells
and cannot be mapped.

There is untold hope
in that no equation exactly
fits a head.

Katherine Gallagher

Oath of Friendship

SHANG YA!
I want to be your friend
For ever and ever without break or decay.
When the hills are all flat
And the rivers are all dry,
When it lightens and thunders in winter,
When it rains and snows in summer,
When Heaven and Earth mingle –
Not till then will I part from you.

Anon. (First century BC)
(trans. Arthur Waley)

Playing a Dazzler

You bash drums playing a dazzler;
I worry a trumpet swaying with it.

You dance, you make a girl's skirt swirl;
I dance, I dance by myself.

You bowl, I lash air and my wicket;
I bowl, you wallop boundary balls.

Your goal-kick beat me between my knees;
my goal-kick flies into a pram-and-baby.

You eat off your whole-pound chocolate cake;
I swell up halfway to get my mate's help.

My bike hurls me into the hedge;
your bike swerves half-circle from trouble.

I jump the wall and get dumped;
you leap over the wall and laugh, satisfied.

I touch the country bridge and walk;
you talk and talk.

You write poems with line-end rhymes;
I write poems with rhymes nowhere or anywhere.

Your computer game screens monsters and gunners;
my game brings on swimmers and courting red-birds.

James Berry

Trying It On

I used to sneak into my sister's room
when she was out.
I pinched her lipstick, made my mirrored mouth
a cherry pout.

One time I found this bronzing tube and creamed
my spotty face.
By break I was a tan-streaked member of
the Asian race.

The Head was mad and wrote a letter home –
my Mam was tamping.
She banned me from the treasure drawers and
left me stamping.

She said, 'No more of that, young brazen miss!'
(like brass, it means).
Instead I tried on heaps of sister-clothes,
her tops and jeans.

When I am sixteen I will be a model,
look so ultra-cool.
It's not fair I can't have stuff of my own
to make boys drool.

I peeked in when our Anne was kissing Dai,
just for some tips.
She caught me, threw a shoe and said,
'You're pushing your luck, you are!'

Jean Gill

The Lie

'I'm not talking to you,' she said.
'You'll just go and put me in one of your poems.'
'No, I won't,' I said.

Alan Durant

Take Note

Elephants and
Hippos are banned.
Punk Rock too
Might get out of hand.
And there is absolutely no room
For desert islands –
They tend to be too huge and heavy,
Matted with hairy trees
And slow-grown undergrowth.

Sloths are not permitted
To hang about –
Trout are considered
To be slippery customers
And will not be allowed entry.

Spiders and woodlice will be
Guaranteed new housing.
Curtains must keep silent
And carpets be sworn to secrecy.
Yoghurt will not be allowed –
While cities are considered
Too much of a crowd.

Double Decker buses
Would look out of place
And faces with fangs

That drip blood are barred.
Mud would be hard
To contain –
And any use of the word 'mathematics'
Is a calculated risk.

Brothers and sisters
Are frisked before entry and
Adults who throw
Their mouths about
Will not even be considered.

Take note –
And be warned –
This is my room.

Pie Corbett

Uncle Ivor

There was the white-painted woodwork
The house with the plum-tree lawn
And the door opening wide for the
Warm Welsh welcome of
'Hello, Kathleen!'
The hug and kiss for my mother,
The bustling fussiness of
Loud greetings, handshakes
Shoulder hugs and backslaps
For my older brothers
By Uncle Ivor

Bestower of gifts –
York station steam engines,
Castle Museum dungeons,
York Minster towers,
River Ouse boat trips,
Rowntrees chocolate misshapes and . . .

Suddenly the door closes in my face
As my greeting turn comes:
'We don't want the likes of you, thank you!'
And, at seven years of age, I am left
Stranded on the doorstep
Not quite sure if it's a joke.

Chris Eddershaw

from *Snap Shots*

the first time i saw
my mum take her teeth out
i thought it was wonderful
must have been five
and i tried and i tried
but i couldn't get my teeth
to slippin' and slide out
no way could i capture
the click an' no doubt
as she took her teeth out
the matter o' fact
as she clacked 'er teeth back.

Labi Siffre

Exits

Our Mum is so theatrical.
When she leaves our house
she takes one encore after another.

'Bye Mum,' we say
as she exits.

And then we stay
exactly where we are
and wait
for one, perhaps two minutes
till there's a rat-a-tat-tat
on the door.

And when we open it
there's Mum,
handbag wide open
stirring the contents
till she says,
'I can't find my keys.'

And in she'll come
then out again
with the keys in her hand

And then we stay
exactly where we are
and wait
for one, perhaps two minutes,
till there's a key in the lock
and this time it's
'Oh, I forgot,
there's a cake in the cupboard
if you're hungry . . .'

Our Mum is so theatrical,
her encores
mathematical,
two at least,
sometimes more
before she's finally
out the door
and away.

Brian Moses

In the Garden Sat a Hat

I looked out of the bedroom window.
Cloud, rain, wind and no one about
on this blustery Sunday morning.

But, in the middle of the garden
sat a hat, a gentleman's hat, a Trilby hat.
And it was not mine, not mine indeed.

It sat there like a cowering animal;
lonely, afraid, with rain lashing down on it
and the wind lifting its rim so slightly.

Perhaps it fell from an angel's head as it
swooped over our house in the middle night.
Maybe it was left there by a fairy gardener.

Then again the wind might have blown it
off the white head of a very well dressed ghost.
The owner murdered and buried in my garden?

I dressed and went downstairs to fetch the hat.
It was soaked through but it felt light as air.
Nowadays I wear it when I go to the Post Office.

People say:
'It suits you, that hat. Where did you get it?'
'Oh, it's just a hat I've had for years;
it was a present from old Jack Strawberry.'

John Rice

At Cider Mill Farm

I remember my uncle's farm
Still in mid-summer
Heat hazing the air above the red roof tops
Some cattle sheds, a couple of stables
Clustered round a small yard
Lying under the hills that stretched their long back
Through three counties.

I rolled with his dogs
Among the hay bales
Stacked high in the barn he built himself
During a storm one autumn evening
Tunnelled for treasure or jumped with a scream
From a pirate ship's mast into the straw
Burrowed for gold and found he'd buried
Three battered Ford cars deep in the hay.

He drove an old tractor that sweated oil
In long black streaks down the rusty orange
It chugged and whirred, coughed into life
Each day as he clattered across the cattle grids
I remember one night my cousin and I
Dragging back cows from over the common
We prodded the giant steaming flanks
Pushed them homeward through the rain
And then drank tea from huge tin mugs
Feeling like farmers.

He's gone now, he sold it
But I have been back for one last look
To the twist in the lane that borders the stream
Where Mary, Ruth and I once waded
Water sloshing over our wellies
And I showed my own children my uncle's farm,
The barn still leaning over the straw,
With for all I know three battered Ford cars
Still buried beneath it.

David Harmer

Hide and Seek

You lose your father after dark
one Saturday, somewhere between
    home and Singleton Park.

Huge cars roar past: you've never seen
    shapes that black, eyes that bright.
Where will they go? Where have they been?

    Your dad's nowhere in sight
and yet you never closed your eyes.
    Now you are deep inside the night –

though night is only morning in disguise
    – and every street light stares
at you, or soaks you in its dyes.

You're out alone, but no one cares . . .
and then you hear the paws, the steamy breath
of wolves, of grizzly bears.

Stephen Knight

The Sick Rose

O Rose, thou art sick,
The invisible worm
That flies in the night
In the howling storm

Has found out thy bed
Of crimson joy,
And his dark secret love
Does thy life destroy.

William Blake

The Quarrel

I quarrelled with my brother
I don't know what about,
One thing led to another
And somehow we fell out.
The start of it was slight,
The end of it was strong,
He said he was right,
I knew he was wrong!

217

We hated one another.
The afternoon turned black.
Then suddenly my brother
Thumped me on the back,
And said, 'Oh, *come* along!
We can't go on all night –
I was in the wrong.'
So he was in the right.

Eleanor Farjeon

A Poison Tree

I was angry with my friend:
I told my wrath, my wrath did end.
I was angry with my foe:
I told it not, my wrath did grow.

And I watered it in fears,
Night and morning with my tears;
And I sunned it with smiles,
And with soft deceitful wiles.

And it grew both day and night,
Till it bore an apple bright;
And my foe beheld it shine,
And he knew that it was mine,

And into my garden stole.
When the night had veiled the pole:
In the morning glad I see
My foe outstretched beneath the tree.

William Blake

Cross Words

```
                t
t      w h a m
r i p      r      d
i        a  t w i s t          s   s   s c r a p
p o k e    s h g u        s l a n g   h
   i    s h o u t    g r i p    a a     u
   b c l a w   m   c     u s p i t    c
w r e c k   e   p u l l    n n    c h o k e
h a   s h a k e    o    s c a      h
a   t   n r      h u r l   h u r t
c   s e   s t a b t    i     l
k   w r e n c h   i    n j
   a   r    o    f s   g r a b
   t   r a v e   f l o g    b a n g
   b   a    e      c      t
   a   n   k n o c k    h i t
   s c r a t c h    u      l e t ' s
   h         f      b e
             f      e
                    s
          m a t e s
```

Gina Douthwaite

A Spell Against the Loosening of the Tongue

Lock up my tongue with a silver key
Guard the secret given me
Wear the key around my neck
Resist the gaudy gossips' beck
And call.

If I give tongue like unruly hounds
And spill the words that lodge in trust:
A plague of ulcers maul my mouth,
My rosy lips be turned to dust.

Judith Green

Touchy

'WHO D'YOU THINK YOU'RE STARING AT?'
The bomber-jacket

on a short fuse
scans the disco crush

The can in his grip
makes a hush

as it crumples. Everybody
finds a different way

to look anywhere else,
not to lock on his eyes.

'WHO D'YOU THINK YOU'RE STARING AT?'
He really needs to know.

Any moment he'll be rattling
someone like a street-collector's tin

with only coppers in it. Then
he'll nut him, drop him limp

at our feet and stare round
at a loss for an answer.

Philip Gross

Quarry

I scratched his hand by accident
God – I'm sorry! I yelled,
my own hand at my mouth in reflex.
But there wasn't any of the blood
that I expected, only a glint
of pink granite that winked
through pale torn skin.
Heart sinking, I guessed then,
beneath his warm exterior,
if I dug deeper,
I'd find a heart of stone.

Janina Ana Karpinska

221

Bullies

With the eye in the back of his head
he sees them coming –

eight-year-old breakers,
baby-hard, baby-soft.

Their space-machine, so elegant
could swallow him,

drown him once and for all
in a dish of air.

No use trying to rewrite the law:
they are the masters –

skills bred in the bone.
He freezes –

they expect it,
though a voice inside him squeaks

I . . . Words cut his tongue,
weigh in his mind like a bruise.

Katherine Gallagher

The Bully Asleep

One afternoon, when grassy
Scents through the classroom crept,
Bill Craddock laid his head
Down on his desk, and slept.

The children came round him:
Jimmy, Roger, and Jane;
They lifted his head timidly
And let it sink again.

'Look, he's gone sound asleep, Miss,'
Said Jimmy Adair;
'He stays up all night, you see;
His mother doesn't care.'

'Stand away from him, children.'
Miss Andrews stooped to see.
'Yes, he's asleep; go on
With your writing, and let him be.'

'Now's a good chance!' whispered Jimmy;
And he snatched Bill's pen and hid it.
'Kick him under the desk, hard;
He won't know who did it.'

'Fill all his pockets with rubbish –
Paper, apple-cores, chalk.'
So they plotted, while Jane
Sat wide-eyed at their talk.

Not caring, not hearing,
Bill Craddock he slept on;
Lips parted, eyes closed –
Their cruelty gone.

'Stick him with pins!' muttered Roger.
'Ink down his neck!' said Jim.
But Jane, tearful and foolish,
Wanted to comfort him.

John Walsh

Ring Home

She's come so far, what can she say?
She's punched her last coin in.
There's a pinball flicker
of connections, then the ansafone:

her mother, the voice
of her whole life so far
sounding cramped in that little
black box, speaking slow

as a hostage in the judder
of a ransom video. *Please
leave your name and your number.
Speak after the tone.*

She can't find the words to explain
to a ghost in a machine
a hundred miles away
in the hall in the house that was home.

Philip Gross

All of Us

All of us are afraid
More often than we tell.

There are times we cling like mussels to the sea-
                                                    wall,
And pray that the pounding waves
Won't smash our shell.

Times we hear nothing but the sound
Of our loneliness, like a cracked bell
From fields far away where the trees are in icy
                                                    shade.

O many a time in the night-time and in the day,
More often than we say,
We are afraid.

If people say they are never frightened,
I don't believe them.

If people say they are frightened,
I want to retrieve them

From that dark shivering haunt
Where they don't want to be,
Nor I.

Let's make of ourselves, therefore, an enormous
                                                    sky
Over whatever
We most hold dear.

And we'll comfort each other,
Comfort each other's
Fear.

Kit Wright

The Window's Eyes

The window's eyes are glazed with constant staring.
Sometimes, the sky is all too bright,
the sun beyond bearing,
at other times the dark that comes at night
seems stuck there and it's getting very late
but you lie awake and wait
for all the stars to creep
across your half closed lids and sleep,

226

while the glass eyes of the houses all look out
reflecting on the streetlights, full of doubt.

George Szirtes

Secret

Tell me your secret.
I promise not to tell.
I'll guard it safely at the bottom of a well.

Tell me your secret.
Tell me, tell me, please.
I won't breathe a word, not even to the bees.

Tell me your secret.
It will be a pebble in my mouth.
Not even the sea can make me spit it out.

John Agard

The Purpose of Angels

You ring, to say you've seen an angel.

In the fibres of grey drizzle
you stand with the phone
pressed to your ear
in an unblessed crowd;
technology crackles and gutters:
   '. . . blue, transparent . . . wings . . .
     hanging above . . . street . . .
      a messenger . . .'

Then the flame steadies
   and I hear you.

               Judith Green

the clouds bunch quietly

   the clouds bunch quietly –
   I wait alone
   after missing the bus

               Gary Hotham

228

High Dive

It feels very lonely, up here against the clouds
and girders of the glass roof. The pool so far away,
framed in flowers of a thousand upturned faces.

Walk to the brink, turn, and carefully
(firm toes gripping this last hold on life)
hang heels in space. Face a blank wall.

Raise arms slowly, sideways, shoulder-high,
silent passion, dream-deep concentration
foretelling every second of the coming flight.

Then with a sudden upward beat of palms,
of arms like wings, gathering more than thought
launch backwards into take-off, into one ball

roll for a quadruple reverse somersault
that at the last split second flicks
open like a switchblade –

feet pointed as in prayer, neat-folded hands
stab the heavens like a dagger, plunge
deep into the pool's azure flesh – without a splash.

James Kirkup

Growler

Like a toad
beneath a suddenly
flipped stone

huffed up
as if about
to sing (but no

sound comes)
yes, it was me.
I was the one

who cracked the bell
of everyone's *hey-*
Ring-A-Ding-Ding-

Sweet-Lovers-Love-the . . .
'Stop!' Miss Carver
clapped her hands.

'Which one of you's
the Growler?' No one
breathed. 'Very well.

Sing on.' And she leaned
very close
all down the line till

230

'Stop!'
She was as small as me
(aged eight)

but sour and sixty,
savage for the love
of her sweet music

I was curdling.
'You!
How *dare* you?

Out!' Down the echoing
hall, all eyes on me . . .
My one big solo.

She died last year.
I hope somebody sang.
Me, I'm still growling.

Philip Gross

The Hate

We began each morning with hymns,
'Lots of wind,' our teacher called
as she wrestled a melody
from the ancient hall piano.

Then we sat and gazed at the front
while the football results were read
and Donald was led in, held by the arm,
a look of alarm on his face.
I didn't know what he'd done,
perhaps he'd stolen or two-fingered
once too often. It must have been serious
in the eyes of God, in the eyes
of our headmistress.

She seemed to think
that boys' backsides were meant to be whacked,
but Donald struggled and lay on the floor
and flapped like a fish out of water.
Even the toughies were terrified
as the slipper rose and fell
a total of eighteen times till it stopped
and Donald stayed locked to the floor.

The piano was open but no one played
as we filed out silent and found our maths.
It stayed on our minds for much of the day
but Donald wouldn't say what he'd done
just shook his head and said nothing.

Our teacher said Donald would be forgiven,
start once again and clean the slate;
but I glimpsed him next day in prayers,
a dreadful look on his face, and I knew
it would take more than Jesus
to wipe away the hate.

Brian Moses

The Visitor

A crumbling churchyard, the sea and the moon;
The waves had gouged out grave and bone;
A man was walking, late and alone . . .

He saw a skeleton white on the ground;
A ring on a bony finger he found.

He ran home to his wife and gave her the ring.
'Oh, where did you get it?' He said not a thing.

'It's the loveliest ring in the world,' she said,
As it glowed on her finger. They slipped off to bed.

At midnight they woke. In the dark outside,
'Give me my ring!' a chill voice cried.

'What was that, William? What did it say?'
'Don't worry, my dear. It'll soon go away.'

'I'm coming!' A skeleton opened the door.
'Give me my ring!' It was crossing the floor.

'What was that, William? What did it say?'
'Don't worry, my dear. It'll soon go away.'

'I'm reaching you now! I'm climbing the bed.'
The wife pulled the sheet right over her head.

It was torn from her grasp and tossed in the air:
'I'll drag you out of your bed by the hair!'

'What was that, William? What did it say?'
'Throw the ring through the window! THROW IT
AWAY!'

She threw it. The skeleton leapt from the sill,
Scooped up the ring and clattered downhill,
Fainter . . . and fainter . . . Then all was still.

Ian Serraillier

The Listeners

'Is there anybody there?' said the Traveller,
Knocking on the moonlit door;
And his horse in the silence champed the grasses
Of the forest's ferny floor;
And a bird flew up out of the turret,
Above the Traveller's head:
And he smote upon the door again a second time;
'Is there anybody there?' he said.
But no one descended to the Traveller;
No head from the leaf fringed sill
Leaned over and looked into his grey eyes,
Where he stood perplexed and still.
And only a host of phantom listeners

That dwelt in the lone house then
Stood listening in the quiet of the moonlight
To that voice from the world of men:
Stood thronging the faint moonbeams on the dark stair,
That goes down to the empty hall,
Hearkening in an air stirred and shaken
By the lonely Traveller's call.
And he felt in his heart their strangeness,
Their stillness answering his cry,
While his horse moved, cropping the dark turf,
'Neath the starred and leafy sky;
For he suddenly smote on the door, even
Louder, and lifted his head: –
'Tell them I came, and no one answered,
That I kept my word,' he said.
Never the least stir made the listeners,
Though every word he spake
Fell echoing through the shadowiness of the still house
From the one man left awake:
Ay, they heard his foot upon the stirrup,
And the sound of iron on stone,
And how the silence surged softly backward,
When the plunging hoofs were gone.

Walter de la Mare

A Smuggler's Song

If you wake at midnight, and hear a horse's feet,
Don't go drawing back the blind, or looking in the street,
Them that ask no questions isn't told a lie.
Watch the wall, my darling, while the Gentlemen go by!
      Five and twenty ponies,
      Trotting through the dark –
      Brandy for the Parson,
      'Baccy for the Clerk;
      Laces for a lady, letters for a spy,
And watch the wall, my darling, while the gentlemen go by!

Running round the woodlump if you chance to find
Little barrels, roped and tarred, all full of brandy-wine,
Don't you shout to come and look, nor use 'em for your
    play.
Put the brushwood back again – and they'll be gone next
    day!

If you see the stable-door setting open wide;
If you see a tired horse lying down inside;
If your mother mends a coat cut about and tore;
If the lining's wet and warm – don't you ask no more!

If you meet King George's men, dressed in blue and red,
You be careful what you say, and mindful what is said.
If they call you 'pretty maid,' and chuck you 'neath the
    chin,
Don't you tell where no one is, nor yet where no one's been!

Knocks and footsteps round the house – whistles after dark –
You've no call for running out till the house-dogs bark.
Trusty's here, and *Pincher*'s here, and see how dumb they
    lie –
They don't fret to follow when the Gentlemen go by!

If you do as you've been told, likely there's a chance,
You'll be given a dainty doll, all the way from France,
With a cap of Valenciennes, and a velvet hood –
A present from the Gentlemen, along o' being good!
      Five and twenty ponies,
      Trotting through the dark –
      Brandy for the Parson,
      'Baccy for the Clerk.
Them that asks no questions isn't told a lie –
Watch the wall, my darling, while the Gentlemen go by!

                         Rudyard Kipling

The Highwayman
Part I

The wind was a torrent of darkness among the gusty trees,
The moon was a ghostly galleon tossed upon cloudy seas,
The road was a ribbon of moonlight over the purple moor,
And the highwayman came riding –
      Riding – riding –
The highwayman came riding, up to the old inn-door.

He'd a French cocked-hat on his forehead, a bunch of lace
    at his chin,
A coat of claret velvet, and breeches of brown doe-skin;
They fitted with never a wrinkle. His boots were up to the
    thigh!
And he rode with a jewelled twinkle,
            His pistol butts a-twinkle.
His rapier hilt a-twinkle, under the jewelled sky.

Over the cobbles he clattered and clashed in the dark inn-
    yard,
He tapped with his whip on the shutters, but all was
    locked and barred;
He whistled a tune to the window, and who should be
    waiting there
But the landlord's black-eyed daughter,
            Bess, the landlord's daughter,
Plaiting a dark red love-knot into her long black hair.

And in the dark old inn-yard a stable-wicket creaked
Where Tim the ostler listened. His face was white and
    peaked.
His eyes were hollows of madness, his hair like mouldy
    hay,
But he loved the landlord's daughter,
            The landlord's red-lipped daughter.
Dumb as a dog he listened, and he heard the robber say –

'One kiss, my bonny sweetheart, I'm after a prize tonight,
But I shall be back with the yellow gold before the
  morning light;
Yet, if they press me sharply, and harry me through the
  day,
Then look for me by moonlight,
        Watch for me by moonlight,
I'll come to thee by moonlight, though hell should bar the
  way.'

He rose upright in the stirrups. He scarce could reach her
  hand,
But she loosened her hair i' the casement! His face burnt
  like a brand
As the black cascade of perfume came tumbling over his
  breast;
And he kissed its waves in the moonlight,
        (Oh, sweet black waves in the moonlight!)
Then he tugged at his rein in the moonlight, and galloped
  away to the west.

Part II

He did not come in the dawning. He did not come at
  noon;
And out o' the tawny sunset, before the rise o' the moon,
When the road was a gipsy's ribbon, looping the purple
  moor,
A red-coat came marching –
        Marching – marching –
King George's men came marching, up to the old inn-door.

They said no word to the landlord. They drank his ale
   instead.
But they gagged his daughter, and bound her, to the foot of
   her narrow bed.
Two of them knelt at her casement, with muskets at their
   side!
There was death at every window;
        And hell at one dark window:
For Bess could see, through her casement, the road that *he*
   would ride.

They had tied her up to attention, with many a sniggering
   jest.
They had bound a musket beside her, with the muzzle
   beneath her breast!
'Now, keep good watch!' and they kissed her. She heard
   the dead man say –
Look for me by moonlight;
      Watch for me by moonlight;
I'll come to thee by moonlight, though hell should bar the
   way!

She twisted her hands behind her; but all the knots held
   good!
She writhed her hands till her fingers were wet with sweat
   or blood!
They stretched and strained in the darkness, and the hours
   crawled by like years,
Till, now, on the stroke of midnight,
      Cold, on the stroke of midnight,
The tip of one finger touched it! The trigger at least was
   hers!

The tip of one finger touched it. She strove no more for the
  rest.
Up, she stood up to attention, with the muzzle beneath her
  breast.
She would not risk their hearing; she would not strive
  again;
For the road lay bare in the moonlight;
        Blank and bare in the moonlight;
And the blood of her veins, in the moonlight, throbbed to
  her love's refrain.

Tlot-tlot; tlot-tlot! Had they heard it? The horse-hoofs
  ringing clear;
Tlot-tlot; tlot-tlot, in the distance! Were they deaf that they
  did not hear?
Down the ribbon of moonlight, over the brow of the hill,
The highwayman came riding,
        Riding, riding!
The red-coats looked to their priming! She stood up,
  straight and still.

Tlot-tlot, in the frosty silence! *Tlot-tlot*, in the echoing
  night!
Nearer he came and nearer. Her face was like a light.
Her eyes grew wide for a moment; she drew one last deep
  breath,
Then her finger moved in the moonlight,
        Her musket shattered the moonlight,
Shattered her breast in the moonlight and warned him –
  with her death.

He turned. He spurred to the west; he did not know who
  stood
Bowed, with her head o'er the musket, drenched with her
  own red blood!
Not till the dawn he heard it, his face grew grey to hear
How Bess, the landlord's daughter,
          The landlord's black-eyed daughter,
Had watched for her love in the moonlight, and died in the
  darkness there.

Back, he spurred like a madman, shouting a curse to the
  sky,
With the white road smoking behind him and his rapier
  brandished high.
Blood-red were his spurs i' the golden noon; wine-red was
  his velvet coat;
When they shot him down on the highway,
          Down like a dog on the highway,
And he lay in his blood on the highway, with the bunch of
  lace at his throat.

And still of a winter's night, they say, when the wind is in
  the trees,
When the moon is a ghostly galleon tossed upon cloudy
  seas,
When the road is a ribbon of moonlight over the purple
  moor,
A highwayman comes riding –
          Riding – riding –
A highwayman comes riding, up to the old inn-door.

Over the cobbles he clatters and clangs in the dark inn-
  yard.
And he taps with his whip on the shutters, but all is locked
  and barred.
He whistles a tune to the window, and who should be
  waiting there
But the landlord's black-eyed daughter,
        Bess, the landlord's daughter,
Plaiting a dark red love-knot into her long black hair.

                                        Alfred Noyes

An Eye of Silver

A Bad Princess

A bad princess stomped through the woods
in a pair of boots
            looking for trouble –
diamond tiara, satin dress, hair an absolute mess,
            ready to bubble.

Imagine her shock and surprise
when she bumped straight into
            her very own double:

A Tree Girl,
with shiny holly-green eyes
and a crown of autumn leaves on her wild head,
the colour of both of their hair.

Don't you dare, screamed Bad,
walk in these Royal woods looking like me!

I shall do as I please, you grumpy old thing,
said Tree.
Give me those emeralds that hang from your ears
or I'll kick you hard
and pinch you meanly.
Then we'll see which one of we two
is cut out
        to be Queenly!

Oh! The bad Princess turned
                    and ran,

ran for her life
into the arms of the dull young Prince
and became his wife.

Carol Ann Duffy

Three

I met a miniature King
by the side of the road,
wearing a crown
and an ermine suit –
important, small,
plump as a natterjack toad.
Kneel! he shrieked, *Kneel for the King!*
Certainly not, I said,
I'll do no such thing.

I saw a Giantess,
tall as a tree.
You'll do for a doll, she bellowed,
just the toy for me!
Into the box! Scream hard! Scream long!
I stared at her mad pond eyes
then skipped away.
Dream on . . .

I bumped into an Invisible Boy – *ouch!* –
at the edge of the field.
Give me a chocolate drop,
said a voice.
What do you say? said I.
Please.
So I did
then stared as it floated mid-air
and melted away.

These are three of the people I met yesterday.

Carol Ann Duffy

Extracts *from* The Tempest

'Caliban's complaint' (Act 1, Scene 2)

This island's mine, by Sycorax my mother,
Which thou tak'st from me. When thou cam'st first,
Thou strok'st me and made much of me, would'st give me
Water with berries in't, and teach me how
To name the bigger light, and how the less,
That burn by day and night; and then I lov'd thee.
And show'd thee all the qualities o' th' isle,
The fresh springs, brine-pits, barren place and fertile.
Curs'd be I that did so! All the charms
Of Sycorax, toads, beetles, bats, light on you!

249

For I am all the subjects that you have,
Which first was mine own king; and here you sty
   me
In this hard rock, whiles you do keep from me
The rest o' th' island.

'Full fathom five' (Act 1, Scene 2)

Full fathom five thy father lies;
Of his bones are coral made;
Those are pearls that were his eyes;
Nothing of him that doth fade,
But doth suffer a sea-change
Into something rich and strange.
Sea-nymphs hourly ring his knell:
Ding-dong,
Hark! now I hear them – ding-dong bell.

'Caliban speaks of the isle' (Act 3, Scene 2)

Be not afeard. The isle is full of noises,
Sounds and sweet airs that give delight and hurt
   not.
Sometimes a thousand twangling instruments
Will hum about mine ears; and sometime voices,
That, if I then had wak'd after long sleep,
Will make me sleep again; and then, in dreaming,
The clouds methought would open and show riches
Ready to drop upon me, that, when I wak'd,
I cried to dream again.

'Where the bee sucks' (Act 5, Scene 1)

Where the bee sucks, there suck I;
In a cowslip's bell I lie;
There I couch when owls do cry.
On the bat's back I do fly
After summer merrily.
Merrily, merrily shall I live now
Under the blossom that hangs on the bough.

William Shakepeare

Thief
from 'Six Go Through the World'

Small things are easy; flowers, what was said,
colour from your hair. Others
need practice. Heat of summers.
The certainty things ever really happened.

While you sleep I rifle whole years,
stories you think you know, names and faces.
Legends behind constellations.
The way back home. Old fears.

You won't see them go, a pause at a railway crossing,
A footpath, what lies beyond the forest.
Smooth skin on your forehead. Breath to run.
Take a look. Most of yesterday is missing.

I admit my limits. Can't undo
that combination lock you keep on your desire
to make words rhyme. The craze for trees.
Barrows in the corners of fields defy me

Though my accomplices, wind and rain,
plunder them all night.
Deep in cathedrals I burgle the dust of saints
on TV make daylight robbery of reputations.

I leer out from women's mirrors,
in libraries fray pages from old books.
Who'll even know the stories are going,
the poems being whittled away?

My one fear is some shadow I might snatch
will be my own. There's too much
world without me. Who'll take
your nightmares then, the fierce despairs

of children, terror of the future? And when
the quest is over who'll be merciful?
Who'll relieve you of your
hunger to go on?

Catherine Fisher

Overheard on a Saltmarsh

Nymph, nymph, what are your beads?
Green glass, goblin. Why do you stare at them?
Give them me.

No.

Give them me. Give them me.

No.

Then I will howl all night in the reeds.
Lie in the mud and howl for them.

Goblin, why do you love them so?

They are better than stars or water,
Better than voices of winds that sing,
Better than any man's fair daughter,
Your green glass beads on a silver ring.

Hush, I stole them out of the moon.

Give me your beads, I desire them.

No.

I will howl in a deep lagoon
For your green glass beads, I love them so.
Give them me. Give them.

No.

Harold Monro

Witches' Chant

Round about the cauldron go:
In the poisoned entrails throw.
Toad, that under cold stone
Days and nights has thirty-one
Swelter'd venom sleeping got,
Boil thou first i' th' charmed pot.
　　Double, double toil and trouble;
　　Fire burn and cauldron bubble.

Fillet of a fenny snake,
In the cauldron boil and bake;
Eye of newt and toe of frog,
Wool of bat and tongue of dog,
Adder's fork and blindworm's sting,
Lizard's leg and owlet's wing.
For a charm of powerful trouble,
Like a hell-broth boil and bubble.
　　Double, double toil and trouble;
　　Fire burn and cauldron bubble.

Scale of dragon, tooth of wolf,
Witch's mummy, maw and gulf
Of the ravin'd salt-sea shark,
Root of hemlock digged i' th' dark . . .
Make the gruel thick and slab;
Add thereto a tiger's chaudron,
For th' ingredients of our cauldron.
      Double, double toil and trouble;
      Fire burn and cauldron bubble.

William Shakespeare
(from Macbeth*)*

Kubla Khan

In Xanadu did Kubla Khan
A stately pleasure-dome decree:
Where Alph, the sacred river, ran
Through caverns measureless to man
Down to a sunless sea.
So twice five miles of fertile ground
With walls and towers were girdled round:
And there were gardens bright and sinuous rills,
Where blossomed many an incense-bearing tree;
And here were forests ancient as the hills,
Enfolding sunny spots of greenery.

But oh! that deep romantic chasm which slanted
Down the green hill athwart a cedarn cover!
A savage place! as holy and enchanted
As e'er beneath a waning moon was haunted
By woman wailing for her demon-lover!
And from this chasm, with ceaseless turmoil seething,
As if this earth in fast thick pants were breathing,
A mighty fountain momently was forced:
Amid whose swift half-intermitted burst
Huge fragments vaulted like rebounding hail,
Or chaffy grain beneath the thresher's flail;
And 'mid these dancing rocks at once and ever
It flung up momently the sacred river.
Five miles meandering with a mazy motion
Through wood and dale the sacred river ran,
Then reached the caverns measureless to man,
And sank in tumult to a lifeless ocean:
And 'mid this tumult Kubla heard from far
Ancestral voices prophesying war!
The shadow of the dome of pleasure
Floated midway on the waves;
Where was heard the mingled measure
From the fountain and the caves.
It was a miracle of rare device,
A sunny pleasure-dome with caves of ice!

A damsel with a dulcimer
In a vision once I saw:
It was an Abyssinian maid,
And on her dulcimer she play'd,

Singing of Mount Abora.
Could I revive within me
Her symphony and song,
To such a deep delight 'twould win me,
That with music loud and long,
I would build that dome in air.
That sunny dome! those caves of ice!
And all who heard should see them there,
And all should cry, Beware! Beware!
His flashing eyes, his floating hair!
Weave a circle round him thrice,
And close your eyes with holy dread,
For he on honey-dew hath fed,
And drunk the milk of Paradise.

Samuel Taylor Coleridge

The Magic Box

I will put in the box

the swish of a silk sari on a summer night,
fire from the nostrils of a Chinese dragon,
the tip of a tongue touching a tooth.

I will put in the box

a snowman with a rumbling belly,
a sip of the bluest water from Lake Lucerne,
a leaping spark from electric fish.

I will put in the box

three violet wishes spoken in Gujarati,
the last joke of an ancient uncle,
and the first smile of a baby.

I will put in the box

a fifth season and a black sun,
a cowboy on a broom stick
and a witch on a white horse.

My box is fashioned from ice and gold and steel,
with stars on the lid and secrets in the corners.
Its hinges are the toe joints
of dinosaurs.

I shall surf in my box
on the great high-rolling breakers of the wild
    Atlantic,
then wash ashore on a yellow beach
the colour of the sun.

Kit Wright

Getting Rid of the Box

The box had five locks
and four false floors,
and a welded-shut door.

And six men carried it
to a nuclear submarine
which burrowed through the ocean

to the first icy suburb
of Antarctica, where no
human marked the ice or snow.

The captain gave the order
to unleash a torpedo
as deep in the ice as it would go,

then in the blast hole
he offloaded the box
and covered it with ice-rocks,

then a second torpedo
brought more ice collapsing
on to the nauseous thing,

and at last he knew
the box's grisly cargo
was as safe as the snow,

and none of that stuff
we'd all crammed in
would ever bother us again.

Matthew Sweeney

In the Time of the Wolf

Who sings the legend?
The mouse in the rafters,
the owl in the forest,
the wind in the mountains,
the tumbling river.

Where can we read it?
In a shadow in the grass,
in the footprint in the sand,
in reflections on the water,
in the fossil in the stone.

How shall we keep it?
In the lake of history,
in the box called memory,
in the voice of the teller,
in the ear of the child.

How will we tell it?
With a tongue of lightning,
with a drum of thunder,
with a strumming of grasses,
with a whisper of wind.

Gillian Clarke

Dazzledance

I have an eye of silver,
I have an eye of gold,
I have a tongue of reed-grass
     and a story to be told.

I have a hand of metal,
I have a hand of clay,
I have two arms of granite
     and a song for every day.

I have a foot of damson,
I have a foot of corn,
I have two legs of leaf-stalk
     and a dance for every morn.

I have a dream of water,
I have a dream of snow,
I have a thought of wildfire
     and a harp-string long and low.

I have an eye of silver,
I have an eye of gold,
I have a tongue of reed-grass
    and a story to be told.

John Rice

A Word is Dead

A word is dead
When it is said,
Some say.
I say it just
Begins to live
That day.

Emily Dickinson

262

Curious Craft

Shallow Poem

I've thought of a poem.
I carry it carefully,
nervously, in my head,
like a saucer of milk;
in case I should spill some lines
before I can put it down.

Gerda Mayer

I Want to Write . . .

I want to write a poem like
    a grotto in the hillside,

limestone carved by ancient water
into shapes like candle wax,

green moss in dark corners
that glows with its own light.

You can sit and hold your breath
and hear
        a drip

in the dark clear pool
you hadn't seen till now.

You can follow its echo
going back   back   back

beneath the hill
as far

as the tingling in your mind
can take you . . .

Philip Gross

Curious Craft

In the boat made of wind
the hold is laden with scents you can't name,
a hint of other weathers, and the itch
of desert sand, and bells, and butterflies,
and voices out of lives and cities
we can see but never touch, because we
are the boat made of wind, and all we can do
is fly. We have to fly.

The boat on stilts
is fastidious, almost too well-bred to touch
the water. My grandmother used to taste
new-fangled food she wasn't sure of
'with long teeth', she said. So the delicate
boat shudders over the world like a pond skater,
wincing when the slick pool's surface puckers
to cling to the touch of its feet.

On the boat made of second thoughts
the crew keeps gazing homewards,
(even the steersman) as if each of them
had dropped something, maybe his heart,
overboard and could still see it bobbing
in the wake, paddling off – like rats
who'd had a premonition and jumped ship
the way old sailors say they do
and never looked back to tell us why.

Philip Gross

Poems in Flight

Brushed ever so lightly
by a poem's passing. Got it,
missed. The poem goes
its way with the rest,
with nowhere to go
but back to the vocabulary
from which it set off.
I wish there were a migration
time for poetry, so nets
could be set up in promising
places. No luck. Poems
have no call-notes, nor have they
set times. They come from where
they have been wintering, seeking

267

for places in which to fashion
the words' nest, high in the boughs
of thought or deep down
in impenetrable darkness.
There are no trappers
of a poem. We only know
when one is about when it has drifted
by us, trailing a fragrance.

R. S. Thomas

What Does Poetry Do?

It nosedives from the top of the fridge
into a bowl of rapids,

it crawls along the floor
and taps you on the knee,

it changes the colour of a room,

it puts great wheezing slices of life
into bun trays, with or without punctuation.

It manages this all by itself.

Chrissie Gittins

One of the Difficulties of Writing a Poem Using Only Nine Words

On to the world's shoulders
Snow falls like dandruff

Snow falls like dandruff
On to the world's shoulders

Like dandruff, snow
Falls on to the world's shoulders

Snow, like dandruff, falls
On to the world's shoulders

On to the world's shoulders
Like dandruff, snow falls

Dandruff like snow
Falls on to the world's shoulders

On to the world's shoulders
Dandruff falls like snow.

Brian Patten

The Robin

I tried to write a poem today,
I tried to make it rhyme,
I tried to get the meaning right
But every single time
I thought I'd got the hang of it,
I thought I'd got it right,
I found I couldn't think of a word
To rhyme with bird
Or, that is, robin.

I didn't want to say
I saw a robin.
It was bobbing
Along and sobbing.
Because it wasn't.

So I started again.

Once, last winter, in the snow,
I was out in the garden
At the bird table,
When I turned round
And saw on the path beside me,
A robin.

It was so close
I could have touched it.
It took my breath away.

I have never forgotten
The red of it
And the white snow falling.

June Crebbin

I Took the Hammer to My Old Desk

I took the hammer to my old desk.
Three whacks broke its long, flat back.

An old-fashioned desk, brown as a branch,
deep scars here and there on its rump.
A sizeable chunk missing from its underbelly.

I took the hammer to my old desk.
A few hefty blows split its thick thighs.

Its newspaper-lined drawers (March 1987)
were full of things that should have been thrown
out ages ago. An empty tin, rusty paper clips.

I took the hammer to my old desk.
Four solid taps separated its legs from its body.

At this desk I have written letters to my children.
I've paid bills, sent emails, signed Christmas cards.
For over 30 years I have written poems at this desk.

271

I took the hammer to my old desk.
One final strike and its whole being was broken.

Woodsplinters and wordshards hurtled through the air.
I gathered them up, carried them downstairs,
placed them on the dinner table, beside the laptop.

I had taken the hammer to my old desk.
Desk became poem.

John Rice

Where Do Ideas Come From?

I once found an idea for a poem
Down the back of the sofa.
It was just out of reach,
Which was annoying,
And I had to reach down
Behind the cushions,
Right up to my elbow,
To fetch it out.

I also found a pound coin.

Roger Stevens

Words

come out
like stars sometimes
and choose the darkest nights
to sparkle in,

are gentle
water-drops suggesting
streams you cannot find the source of
in a landscape where no
water is,

or wasps
behind your back which
suddenly
go silent.

John Mole

Answers to Riddles and Wordplay

Answers to *Short Riddles*, page 59

• the sun
• a comb
• a seed
• age
• a potato
• a human growing up
• a sheep leaving wool

Answer to *Goodnight*, page 60

• a lightbulb

Answer to *How Did He Escape?*, page 62

He rubbed his hands
till they were sore.

He took the saw
and cut the table
right in half.

Two halves make a whole.

So he climbed through the hole.

Once outside –
he cried
till he was hoarse.

He climbed on the horse
and rode away . . .

Answer to *The Tale of the Cleverest Son*, page 64

No scandal –
he bought a candle –
No catch –
he bought a match.
And let light
dispel the gloom
to fill the room.

Answers to *Spelling Riddles*, page 71

• vocabulary
• television
• comedian
• elephant
• knowledge
• afternoons
• impossibility

Glossary of Terms

Acrostic
This is a poetic form that uses the initial letters of a key
word at the beginning of each line, e.g.

Creeps through the darkness,
Along the garden wall,
Tail swaying.

You can also hide the key word within the poem, e.g.

Animal Riddle

Like a small **B**ear
bundles over the dark road,
brushes p**A**st the front gate,
as if she owns the joint,
rolls the **D**ustbin,
like an expert barrel rider,
tucks into yesterday's **G**arbage,
crunches worms for titbits,
wakes us from d**E**ep sleep,
blinks back at torchlight,
our midnight feaste**R**,
ghost-friend,
moon-lit,
zebra bear.

Pie Corbett

Action Verse
These are rhymes that involve an action. They are usually performed for small children!

Adjective
A word that is added or linked to a noun to describe it.
e.g. the *red* dress.

Adverb
A word which adds to a verb, telling us where, when or how. Many end in 'ly'.
e.g. she ran *quickly*.

Alliteration
This is when poets use the same sound close by.
e.g. *the cruel cat cautiously crept by.*
Alliteration is very useful because it draws the reader's attention to the words. It makes the words memorable – often advertisers use alliteration for this reason (Buy a *Ticktock* today). You can have great fun with alliterative sentences by creating Tongue-Twisters. You may know this one:
She sells seashells on the seashore.

Alphabet Poem
This is a poem written using the letters of the alphabet, e.g.
A is an ant,
B is a baboon . . .

Assonance

This is the repetition of vowel sounds close to each other, creating echoes.

e.g. *the figure gave a low groan.*

Ballad

This is a formal poem or song that is meant to be performed aloud. Ballads tell stories, using a regular pattern, usually with verses and a chorus, e.g.

'*O Mary, go and call the cattle home,*
    And call the cattle home,
    And call the cattle home,
    Across the sands of Dee!'
The western wind was wild and dank with foam,
    And all alone went she.

From 'The Sands of Dee' by Charles Kingsley.

Blank Verse

This is poetry that is written with a rhythm and metre but has no rhymes. Shakespeare often wrote in blank verse.

Calligram

This is a picture poem made of letters representing an aspect of the poem. For instance, if the word chosen was 'shake' the writer might write the word using a wobbly typeface, 's h a k e'. In the example below the words are leaning across to reflect the meaning.

The sloping wall.

Chant
This is a rhyme that has a strong beat and rhythm. It can be chanted aloud to good effect.

Choral Poem
A poem for speaking aloud by a whole group.

Cinquain
This was invented by the American poet Adelaide Crapsey – it is rather like a haiku – consisting of five lines, using twenty-two syllables, arranged in a sequence 2, 4, 6, 8, 2. The last line is often a surprise.

Classic Poem
This is a poem that has stood the test of time. Its author may be dead but the poem is considered to be sufficiently memorable still to be printed and read.

Cliché
This is an overused, stale phrase or word combination. e.g. the cotton-wool clouds.

Collage Poem
This is a list poem, where each line adds a new image. Many writers use this technique, e.g.
I remember the waves rushing up the beach.
I remember the gulls dipping over the headland.
I remember the black, jagged rocks . . .

Concrete Poem
This is a sort of shape poem where the design of the words adds extra meaning to the poem; it relies on the layout of the words for full impact. The Scottish poet Ian Hamilton Finlay literally made poems out of stone and put them in his garden!

Consonance
This is the repetition of consonants that are close to each other, to create echoes.
e.g. the quick click of his heels . . .

Conversation
This is a poem written as if there was a conversation taking place. Often good for performing aloud!

Counting Rhyme
Rhymes that use numbers,
e.g. *One, two, buckle my shoe* . . .

Couplet
Two consecutive, paired lines of poetry, e.g.
Nor I half turn to go yet turning stay,
Remember me when no more day by day

Determiner
A word that tells you more about a noun, e.g.
A dog
Each dog
Every dog
The dog

Eye (or Sight) Rhyme
These are words that look as if they might rhyme but do not.
e.g. cough/through.

Figurative Language
Use of metaphor or simile to create an impression or mood. Figurative language helps to build up a picture in the reader's mind. Poets use it all the time!

Free Verse
Poetry not constrained by metrical or rhyming patterns. (Some would say that sometimes free verse is just an excuse for not working hard at creating a form!)

Haiku
This is a very popular Japanese form of poetry. It is brief, related to the seasons/nature, expresses a sense of awe or insight, written using concrete sense images and not abstractions, in the present tense. It is often written as three lines, of seventeen syllables arranged in a sequence 5, 7, 5, though not necessarily. A verbal snapshot, capturing the essence of a moment/scene. Some haiku are only a line or two. The idea is to capture a moment, e.g.

Flies stalk the cup's rim
Washing their hands, fidgeting
In the sullen heat.

Half-rhyme
These are words which almost rhyme.
e.g. grip/grab.

Homonym
A word with the same spelling as another, but a different meaning.
e.g. the *calf* was eating/my *calf* was aching.

Pronunciation may be different.
e.g. a *lead* pencil/the dog's *lead*.

Idiom
A phrase often used that is not meant literally. Its meaning is understood by the people who use it, but cannot be inferred from knowledge of the individual words.
e.g. *over the moon, under the weather, thick as two short planks.*

Imagery
This is when you are using language to create a vivid sensory image or picture in the reader's mind. This is done with similes and metaphors but also by carefully selecting the right word.

Internal Rhyme

This is when the poet puts rhymes within lines, e.g.

Lizard cars cruise by.

Their radiators *grin*.

Thin headlights stare . . .

Kenning

This is a sort of riddle. It was used in Old English and Norse poetry to name something without using its name, e.g. mouse catcher (cat). The Anglo Saxons named their swords in this way, e.g. *bone cruncher*.

Limerick

This is a popular form of funny poetry that is actually not easy to write! You need a pattern consisting of five lines. These lines follow a thirty-six-syllable count in a sequence of 8, 8, 6, 6, 8 with rhyme scheme AABBA.

List Poem

This is a poem that is written rather like a list, using the same repeating phrase to introduce each idea, e.g.

I saw a fish on fire.

I saw a bird swim in oil.

I saw . . .

Metaphor

Metaphors are rather like similes, except in a simile you say that one thing is like another. In a metaphor you just say that one thing IS another – so you are writing about something as if it was something else. 'The moon is like a smile' is a simile. 'The moon is a smile' is a metaphor.

Metre
This is the term used to describe the organization of poetry by the pattern of regular rhythm.

Monologue
This is when a character speaks aloud. Monologues are found in plays but some poems are written to be spoken aloud by a character.

Narrative Poem
This is quite simply a story poem. Ballads are a form of narrative poem.

Nonsense Poem
This is poetry that uses nonsense words (*'Twas brillig and the slithy toves*) or writes about nonsensical events (*We put on our pigeons and swam through the custard*).

Noun
A noun is the name of a thing, person, place or idea.

Onomatopoeia
These are words that sound like their meaning.
e.g. *the busy bee buzzes*.

Oral Poem
This is a poem that has been passed down through the
generations by word of mouth.

Performance Poem
This is a poem intended for performance. Often direct and
lively, using rhythm and rhyme. Great fun to join in with.
Of course, most poems can be performed!

Personification
This is a form of metaphor and great fun to write. It is
when you take an object and pretend it has come alive –
rather like sprinkling Disney dust on to broomsticks so
that they get up and start dancing, e.g.
The wind moaned.
The trees stooped down.
The bushes whispered.

Playground Chant/Rhyme
This is a rhyme that children tell in the playground. It is
often used for skipping, clapping, ball-bouncing games,
ring games and dipping.

Powerful Verb
A powerful verb draws the attention of the reader to the
action. It brings energy to the writing by being more
extreme and descriptive, e.g.
'Get out!' she *said* loudly.
'Get out!' she *screamed*.

Prayer
Words spoken to a god.

Pun
This is a play on words, where a word has two meanings.
e.g. the book is not red/the book is not read.

Rap
This is a lively form of poetry that uses strong rhythm and
rapid pace. It is often performed with music and is rather
like rapid, rhyming speech.

Refrain
This is a repeated chorus.

Renga
These are a series of haiku that are linked together. Each
haiku picks up on a link from the previous one. Sometimes
written by different poets to form a series.

Rhyme
These are words that make the same end sounds, e.g.
dig/fig. Half-rhymes are words that almost rhyme, e.g.
slip/sleep. End rhymes fall at the end of the lines in poetry.
Internal rhymes come in the middle of the lines. Eye
rhymes look as if they should rhyme but do not, e.g.
cough/through.

Rhythm
Poems should have rhythm so that the poem is memorable. Rhythm is the more or less regular alternation of light and heavy beats in speech or music to provide a beat.

Riddle
A form of poetry where the subject is hidden and the reader has to guess what is being written about.

Shape Poem
This is a poem that is written in a shape. The shape usually reflects the subject of the poem.

Simile
Similes are used a lot by poets. A simile is when you are saying that one thing is like another, to create a picture in the reader's mind. There are two sorts of simile:
1. Using like, e.g. a saddle *like* a mushroom.
2. Using as, e.g. as slow *as* grass growing.

Song
Words that are intended to be accompanied by music. They often have several verses with a repeated chorus in between.

Sonnet
This is a special form of poetry. It was popular with Italian poets, and began in the thirteenth century. It is a poem of fourteen lines, often following a rhyme scheme.

Surrealism
This is a form of writing that is rather crazy and dream-like – where all sorts of impossible things happen.

Syllabic Poem
Syllabic verse is organized by the pattern of syllables per line.

Syllable
Each beat in a word is a syllable.
e.g. *cat* has one syllable but *kitten* has two (kit-ten).

Synonym
Words which have the same, or very similar, meaning, e.g. wet/damp. Avoids overuse of any word; adds variety.

Tanka
This is a Japanese form based on haiku with two additional lines. Traditionally, when a member of the Japanese court wrote a haiku, the receiver would add two extra lines and return it. It uses a pattern of 5, 7, 5, 7, 7 syllables.

Thin Poem
A shape poem written down or across the page with only a few letters or words per line so that it is thin!

Tongue-twister
These are short lines which alliterate or rhyme. They are often very hard to say, especially when repeated quickly, e.g. unique, New York.

Traditional Rhyme
This is a rhyme that has been known for many years. Many of them are nursery rhymes.

Verb
A word or group of words which names an action or state of being. A Doing Word.

Word Puzzle
A range of word games, often in poetic form.

A–Z of Advice for Young Poets

Audience – present poems by performing, making posters, post-its, use email or stick them in a bottle and let them float away.

Brainstorm – look or think about your subject – write quickly. Cherry pick the best ideas. Train the brain to be quick – and remember – the first thought is not always the best!

Concentrate – learn to look carefully. When writing, blot everything else out. Write furiously.

Decide – writing is about choosing words and ideas. Read your work aloud to see and hear how it sounds. Listen to your own writing as if you had never heard it before.

Experiment – try out different words and combinations. Be brave and try for new combinations – use 'cockerel lava' rather than 'red lava'.

Feelings – write about what moves you. It must matter.

Grow – let poems have time to grow. Come back to them after a while and see how they sound!

Habit – keep on practising; write every day. Don't worry about 'getting it right' – 'get it written', then go back over it!

Imagine – take what you know and invent a bit; play 'what if . . .' or 'supposing'. Cars could break-dance and telegraph poles pick teeth.

Juggle – keep throwing the words up into the air, testing them out.

Know – write about what you know about – interests and obsessions.

Look – become a close observer of the world.

Mimic – notice how other writers gain their effects – use their patterns for practice. Read daily and learn good poems – let beautiful language live forever in your mind.

Notebook – keep a notebook to jot down observations, ideas, and words, things people say, funny things, rhythms and . . . wrestle with words.

Opposites – try words and ideas that conflict – 'loud silences' and 'soft granite'.

Play – play with ideas, so that in the window you see a tulip blossom, so that the moon grins and the sun is a giant gobstopper.

Question – interrogate the world, make the world speak. Ask tigers who made them and why the stars are so silent. Then reply.

Recreate – use words to preserve your experience – to recreate the world. To explain yourself to the world and the world to yourself.

Secrets – use your imagination to discover the secret world – of stones and snakes . . .

Trim – avoid using too many words or they'll cancel each other out.

Unique – find your own ideas and fresh combinations.

Voice/s – try writing as if you were a creature, an object or someone else, write in role – and give the world a voice.

Word hoard – get in the habit of collecting and tasting the flavour of words.

X-ray – look so hard that you can see to the heart.

Yourself – put yourself into your poems as well as the subject.

Zeal – write with energy, enjoyment and celebration.

A–Z of Poetry Reading Ideas

Assembly – hold a poetry assembly where each class performs poems.

Buy words – which words would you buy or borrow from a poem? Keep a notebook to store tasty words.

Cut up and close reading – cut up a poem for someone else to reassemble – by word, line or verse. Or, cut out words and leave spaces to be filled.

Drawing – illustrate a poem – create poem posters.

Enthusiasm – discuss what you liked in a poem, what you didn't like – draw up a desert island list of top ten poems or poets. Hold a vote across the school.

Feelings – read and discuss what poems make you feel and think. Write down or share your first impressions.

Gossip – chat about poets and poems. Hold regular 'recommendation' sessions where you promote a poet or poem that you think others will enjoy.

Highlights – which are the highlights of a poem? Which is a poet's best poem and why? Use a highlighter to identify key words or lines.

Imitate – imitate poetic ideas or patterns and write a poem yourself.

Journals – keep a poetry journal – each week stick in a new poem that you like.

Know it by heart – learn poems by heart. Chant, perform and sing poems out loud.

Letters – write to poets . . . or to characters in their poems.

Memories – what memories does a poem stir – what do you see in your mind, what does it remind you of?

Newspaper headlines – create a newspaper headline and article about a poem or what is happening in a poem, especially narrative poetry.

Organize – a poetry reading or poetry day. Invite poets into school for book weeks or arts festivals.

Performance – perform poems – make tapes and videos. Send these to other classes or schools.

Question – ask questions about poems – what puzzles you? What are you not certain about? Discuss mysteries. Remember – not everything makes sensible sense – sometimes poems have to be experienced and not just understood.

Reread – keep rereading a poem to let its meaning creep up on you – and to let the words sink forever into your mind.

Swap – swap poems over. Find one you think your partner would enjoy.

Title – hide the title of a poem – what might the poem be called?

Underline – use a coloured pencil to underline, star or circle parts of a poem that are of interest – likes, dislikes, puzzles or patterns.

Video – video a reading or class performance of a poem. Put on a poetry show.

Weekly – have a poet of the week or month – read their poems each day.

X-ray – put on your X-ray vision when reading – try to see and listen to the heart of a poem.

Yardstick – collect a few poems that act as your poetic yardstick – what is a really good poem by which all others have to be judged – which are the great ones . . . And why?

Zodiac – create a zodiac of poems – one for each star (or month) sign.

Poetry Writing Workshops
Above and Beyond . . .

Try looking at two things in the same glimpse, not one on its own:

Beyond the walls, a tall stone tower . . .

And think how many A . . . and Be . . . words there are in English to help us place things like this . . .

> Beyond the walls, a tall stone tower
> Between the green,
>   a glimpse of pink
> Below the leaves,
>   the eyes of a cat
>   that stops and watches us
>   then stalks and slinks.
>
> Above the trees,
>   mud-grey clouds rushing
> After we say 'Hush!'
>   the voice of a bird
> Among the leaves
>   and clouds and flowers
>   Susan frowns . . . then grins
>   as she finds the right word.

Try . . .

Beyond . . . Below . . . Beside . . . Before . . . Between . . .
   Behind . . .
Above . . . Among . . . Against . . . Around . . . After . . .

And other linking words like:
Through . . . Over . . . Under . . . Outside . . . Inside . . .

Lines made like this could start whole mini-poems of their
own – e.g.

            Behind the garden thunder clouds
                of rhododendrons rise up
                      ready to burst
                       with stormy
                          pink.

                                            Philip Gross

Dragons' Wood

We didn't see dragons
in Dragons' Wood
but we saw

where the dragons had been.

We saw tracks in soft mud
that could only have been left
by some sharp-clawed creature.

We saw scorched earth
where fiery dragon breath
had whitened everything to ash.

We saw trees burnt to charcoal.
We saw dragon dung
rolled into boulders.

And draped from a branch
we saw sloughed off skin,
scaly, still warm . . .

We didn't see dragons
in Dragons' Wood,
but this was the closest
we'd ever been

to believing.

Brian Moses

There is an actual Dragons' Wood, which is part of The Enchanted Forest at Groombridge Place in Kent. It was after a visit here that I wrote this poem. The wood was gloomy and it was easy to imagine that such creatures might dwell there. The poem doesn't rhyme but it has a pattern and a rhythm through the repetition of *We didn't see . . .* and *We saw . . .*

Explain that the children are going to write a poem of their own that will be structured in a similar way to 'Dragons' Wood'. It will involve a fantasy creature and setting. Look at the poem again, and at how the lines in the poem have been split up. Look also at the similarity between the first verse of the poem and the penultimate verse.

Listing Ideas

Begin by listing different creatures – mermaids, witches, wizards, ogres, giants, trolls, unicorns, etc. Then make a second list of places where these creatures might be found – mountain, shipwreck, valley, cave, wood, castle, chasm, swamp, and so on. Now try to combine a creature with a place to make up a title for the poem: Mermaids' Shipwreck, Wizards' Wood, Unicorn Valley.

Teacher Demonstration

Choose a subject for a class poem on the board and write out the first verse:

> We didn't see mermaids
> in Mermaids' Shipwreck
> but we saw
> where mermaids had been.

Point out how the next verse will begin with *We saw* . . . and ask for ideas relating to the evidence for mermaids. Add the most interesting ones to the poem.

> We saw a golden comb
> with strands of silver hair
> that could only have been abandoned
> by a beautiful lady.

Continue with further verses beginning, *We saw* . . . until the last verse. Here children may wish to imitate the ending of 'Dragons' Wood', but it should be emphasized that if someone has an idea of their own that they'd like to try out, then this is always an option. There is no point in making this exercise a straitjacket for the more imaginative child who may wish to go off in a direction that will prove equally worthwhile.

Brian Moses

What is . . . the Sun?

the Sun is an orange dinghy
   sailing across a calm sea

it is a gold coin
   dropped down a drain in Heaven

the Sun is a yellow beach ball
   kicked high into the summer sky

it is a red thumbprint
   on a sheet of pale blue paper

the Sun is a milk bottle's gold top
   floating in a puddle

Wes Magee

Choose a subject (eg: clouds, or the Moon,
or stars, or a garden pond) and see if you
can create some 'word pictures' (or images).

Keep the same 2-lines-per-verse pattern in your poem.
Think of all the things your subject looks 'like', for
example . . .

Clouds are the clippings
   from God's white beard.

or . . .

The Moon is a bruised banana
lying in a black plastic fruit bowl.

Wes Magee

Shakespeare

One cold summer's evening, we were watching an outdoor
production of *A Midsummer Night's Dream* when I noticed
the lines:

I must go seek some dew-drops here
And hang a pearl in every cowslip's ear
(Act 2, Scene 1, 14–15)

I began wondering what other tasks a fairy or imp might
have to accomplish. While the play was continuing, I began
to note down some ideas.

There is so much to do –
I must sprinkle flecks of frost
On the crisp autumn leaves.
I must seize the hiss of an adder
And hang dew on a spider's web.
I must help the blind mole
Build pyramids of earth.
I must sharpen blades of grass
And put freckles on a child's face.

I must howl with the gale
And dance with the March hare
On the whale-backed hillside.
I must catch the silvery light
That slips from the moon's white face.
I must push green shoots
Through the stubborn earth
And ride on the bumblebee's back.
I must polish the salmon's scales
Till they shine like sunlight.
I must tip dreams into the lover's ear
So that he can hear his wishes . . .

Using lines from Shakespeare or any other great writer can often act as a way into internalizing memorable language as well as a catalyst for children's creativity. For instance:

In nature's infinite book of secrecy
A little I can read . . .
(*Antony and Cleopatra*, Act 1, Scene 2, 10–11)

In summer's burning book of shame
A shimmer I can read . . .
In winter's frozen book of death
A silence I can read . . .
In time's ticking book of terror
A future I could not find . . .
In the cloud's soft book of rain
A fog smothered my view . . .

Hamid (10 years old)

Here are a few more lines that I have tried with children as a basis for their own poems:

O word of fear (Love's Labour's Lost)
A killing frost (Henry VIII)
This is a brave night to cool a courtesan. (King Lear)
But soft, methinks I scent the morning air. (Hamlet)
Peace! – how the moon sleeps . . . (The Merchant of
    Venice)
Swift, swift, you dragons of the night. (Cymbeline)
The ox hath therefore stretched his yoke in vain.
    (A Midsummer Night's Dream)
I know a bank where the wild thyme blows,
Where oxlips and the nodding violet grows . . .
    (A Midsummer Night's Dream)

The teacher-poet Fred Sedgwick has written an excellent book about paying homage to Shakespeare through writing poems based on lines from the plays. The book contains many teaching ideas and examples of children's poems (*Shakespeare and the young writer*, Routledge, 1999). Anyone interested in children's creative writing will find the book both inspiring and practical.

Pie Corbett

Poetry Slams

Some schools hold an annual poetry slam. Children can perform in groups or individually. Time will need to be given to practising and the children should think about the fundamentals of performance:

- Speak your poem clearly
- Make sure the volume is loud enough to be heard
- Use expression and rhythm
- Vary volume, pace and expression for effect
- Use dramatic pauses
- Use simple movement or percussion.

To judge the slam you will need a panel of judges who mark out of a hundred, each focusing on one of the following elements:

- The performance
- The quality of the poem (if written by the performers)
- The volume of the audience's response.

Performance poems, rapid rhymes and rapping lend themselves to slams.

Buy this poem

This poem's up for sale,
It's ready in the frame.
It's got all the things
A poem should contain.

It's got a handsome hero
Saving those in danger,
A love interest resulting in
A baby in a manger.

It's got rhythm, rhyme and skills
And a pack of wolves that kills,
Liquid supersonic metre,
Duplicating by the litre.

The comic duo are your mates,
The criminals you love to hate.
The narrator, who's quite a bore,
The interval, the half-time score.

This poem is for sale,
'Come on' –
This poem is so lovable,
           Incredible,
              Spreadable,
                 Edible.

In fact forget it.
Just put away your money, funny honey.
'Cos I don't want your wealth,
                your health,
                      to be left on the shelf.
This poem goes to one who deserves it.
And that is 'myself'.

Teddy Corbett

Index of Poem Types by Year Group

Year 3

Year 4

Index of Poem Types by Year Group

Index of Poem Types by Year Group

Index of Poem Types by Year Group

Year 5

Index of Poem Types by Year Group

Index of First Lines

Index of Poets

328

Index of Poets

Index of Poets

Acknowledgements

The compiler and publisher would like to thank the following for permission to use copyright material:

John Agard, 'Secret' from *Another Day on Your Foot*, Macmillan Children's Books (1996), 'Rat Race', all by permission of the Caroline Sheldon Literary Agency on behalf of the author; **Moniza Alvi**, 'Map of India' from *Carrying My Wife*, Bloodaxe Books (2000); **Les Baynton**, 'Our Street', by permission of the author; **James Berry**, 'Goodbye Now', ''Bye Now' and 'Playing a Dazzler', by permission of the author; **Clare Bevan**, 'Playground Song', by permission of the author; **Valerie Bloom**, 'December' and 'The Visitor' from *Whoop an' Shout!*, Macmillan Children's Books (2003), 'Whose Dem Boots' and 'Goodbye (Cinquain)' from *The World Is Sweet*, Bloomsbury Children's Books (2000), all reprinted by permission of the author; **Ann Bonner**, 'Gorilla' from *Green Poems*, Oxford University Press (1999), 'Beach' from *Stories for Bedtime*, Collins (1979), all by permission of the author; **Joseph Bruchac**, 'Birdfoot's Grampa' from *Entering Onondaga* (1975), by permission of Barbara S. Kouts Literary Agency; **Dave Calder**, 'Where?', by permission of the author; **James Carter**, 'Icy Morning Haikus' and 'Talking Time', by permission of the author; **Tony Charles**, 'Rabbit and Dragon', by permission of the author; **Debjani Chatterjee**, 'Look at the Cloud-Cat . . .' from *Masala: Poems from India, Bangladesh, Pakistan and Sri Lanka*, Macmillan Children's Books (2005); **Gillian Clarke**, 'In the Time of the Wolf' from *The Animal Wall*, Pont Books (1999), by permission of the author; **David Constantine**, 'Coltsfoot' from *Collected Poems*, Bloodaxe Books (2000); **Teddy Corbett**, 'Clouds', by permission of the author; **John Cotton**, 'Nature's Numbers' and 'Listen', by permission of Peggy Cotton; **Sue Cowling**, 'Alien Lullaby' from *The Works 2*, Macmillan Children's Books (2002), by permission of the author; **June Crebbin**, 'Making the Countryside' and 'The Robin' from *The Crocodile is Coming*, Walker Books (2005), 'Butterfly' by permission of the author; **Walter de la Mare**, 'The Listeners' from *The Complete Poems of Walter de la Mare* (1969), by permission of the Literary Trustees of Walter de la Mare and the Society of Authors as their representative; **Jan Dean**, 'Midnight' from *Wallpapering the Cat*, Macmillan Children's Books (2003); **Emanuel Di Pasquale**, 'Rain', by permission of the author; **Gina Douthwaite**, 'Pheasant', 'Snout Doing', 'Maze', 'Sunset', and 'Cross Words', by permission of the author; **Carol Ann Duffy**, 'The Oldest Girl in the World', 'A Bad Princess' and 'Three'from *The Oldest Girl in the World*, by permission of Faber and Faber Ltd; **Helen Dunmore**, 'Pomegrantes do not Feel Pain', 'Hedgehog Hiding at Harvest in Hills above Monmouth', 'Country

Acknowledgements

Darkness', 'For Francesca' and 'Mid-Winter Haiku', by permission of A. P. Watt Ltd on behalf of the author; **Alan Durant**, 'The Lie', by permission of The Agency (London) on behalf of the author; **Chris Eddershaw**, 'Wolf', 'May-Bugs' and 'Uncle Ivor', by permission of the author; **Eleanor Farjeon**, 'The Quarrel', by permission of David Higham Associates on behalf of the estate of the author ; **John Foster**, 'The Name of the Game' from *Crack Another Yolk*, Oxford University Press (1996), by permission of the author; **Katherine Gallagher**, 'Tanka' from *The Unidentified Flying Omelette*, Hodder (2000), 'A Girl's Head' from *Fish-rings on Water*, Forest Books (1989), 'Bullies' from *Them and Us*, Bodley Head (1993), 'Silly Shifts', all by permission of the author; **Chrissie Gittins**, 'What Does Poetry Do?', by permission of the author; **Judith Green**, 'The Grasshopper Glass Experiment', 'Hollyhock', 'Peppermint', 'Christmas Eve. The mice go to Midnight Mass', 'Springwind', 'Extract from a letter containing two gold maple leaves, 1915', 'A Spell Against the Loosening of the Tongue' and 'The Purpose of Angels', all by permission of the author; **Philip Gross**, 'The Cat's Muse', 'What to Call a Jackdaw', 'Jack's Nature Study', 'Air Bubble', 'Shiver My Timbers', 'Rain in the Rhondda', 'Small Dawn Song', 'The Oubliette', 'Touchy', 'Ring Home', 'Growler', 'I Want to Write . . .', 'Curious Craft', by permission of Faber and Faber Ltd; **David Harmer**, 'South to North; 1965' and 'At Cider Mill Farm', by permission of the author; **Miroslav Holub**; 'A Dog in the Quarry' from *Miroslav Holub: Selected Poems*, translated by Ian Milner, Penguin Books (1969), 'The door' and 'A boy's head' from *Poems Before & After: Collected English Translations*, translated by Ian Milner and George Theiner, Bloodaxe Books (1990); **Libby Houston**, 'Black Dot' from *All Change*, Oxford University Press (1993), by permission of the author; **Langston Hughes**, 'Autumn Thought' from *Collected Poems of Langston Hughes*, Alfred A. Knopf Inc., by permission of David Higham Associates Ltd; **Ted Hughes**, 'A Riddle', 'Leaves' and 'The Warm and the Cold', by permission of Faber and Faber Ltd; **Jackie Kay**, 'Old Tongue', by permission of the author; **Stephen Knight**, 'A Saucerful of Milk' and 'Hide and Seek' from *Sardines and Other Poems*, Young Picador (2005); **George MacBeth**, 'Fourteen Ways of Touching the Peter' from *Collected Poems 1958-1982*, Hutchinson (1989); **Roger McGough**, 'The Sound Collector' from *You Tell Me*, Viking Kestrel (1979), by permission of Peters, Fraser and Dunlop Group Ltd on behalf of the author; **Andrew Matthews**, 'Cat Began' from *Paws and Claws*, Hutchinson Children's Books (1995); **Gerda Mayer**, 'Shallow Poem' from *Bernini's Cat*, Iron Press (1999), by permission of the author; **Adrian Mitchell**, 'Rat It Up' and 'Yes', reprinted by permission of Peters, Fraser and Dunlop Group Ltd on behalf of the author (Educational Health Warning! Adrian Mitchell asks that none of his poems be used in connection with any examinations whatsoever); **John Mole**, 'Words' from *Hot Air*, Hodder (1996), by permission of the author; **Harold Monro**, 'Overheard on a Saltmarsh' from *Collected Poems*, by permission of Gerald Duckworth and Company Ltd;

Acknowledgements

Michaela Morgan, 'Blake's Tyger – revisited' from *Through a Window*, Longman (1995), by permission of the author; **Brian Morse**, 'My Cat Syllable' and 'Cat in the Window' from *A Slice of Sun*, Dagger Press (2003), by permission of the author; **Brian Moses**, 'A Stick Insect' from *I Wish I Could Dine with a Porcupine*, Hodder (2000), 'December Moon' and 'The Hate' from *Barking Back at Dogs*, Macmillan Children's Books (2000), 'Exits', all by permission of the author; **Brian Patten**, 'Not Only', 'Still Winter', 'A Boat in the Snow' and 'One of the Difficulties of Writing a Poem Using Only Nine Words', by permission of Rogers, Coleridge & White; **Taufiq Rafat**, 'The Mango Tree' from *Poetry*, by permission of the author; **James Reeves**, 'Slowly' and 'The Sea', by permission of the Laura Cecil Literary Agency on behalf of the estate of the author; **John Rice**, 'This Morning I Have Risen Early' from *The Dream of Night Fishers*, Scottish Cultural Press (1998), 'Sunfire' from *Bears Don't Like Bananas*, Simon & Schuster (1991), 'Dazzledance' from *Rice, Pie and Moses*, Macmillan Children's Books (1995), 'In the Garden Sat a Hat' and 'I Took the Hammer to My Old Desk', all by permission of the author; **Vernon Scannell**, 'The Apple-Raid', by permission of the author; **Ian Serraillier**, 'The Visitor', by permission of the estate of Ian Serraillier; **Matt Simpson**, 'Walking a Friend's Dog' from *The Pig's Thermal Underwear*, Headland Publications (1993), by permission of the author; **Darren Stanley**, 'Lizards' and 'Rupa's Hand', by permission of the author; **Roger Stevens**, 'Where Do Ideas Come From?' from *I Did Not Eat the Goldfish*, Macmillan Children's Books (2002); **Matthew Sweeney**, 'Getting Rid of the Box' from *Up On the Roof*, Faber and Faber Ltd (2001), by permission of the author; **George Szirtes**, 'The Refrigerator's Belly', 'The Rain's Feet' and 'The Window's Eyes', by permission of the author; **Nick Toczek**, 'They're Out There' from *Dragons!*, Macmillan Children's Books (2005), by permission of the author; **David Whitehead**, 'I Ask You!' from *Poems for Year 3*, Macmillan Children's Books (2002); **William Carlos Williams**, 'This Is Just to Say' and 'The Red Wheelbarrow' from *The Collected Verse of William Carlos Williams*, Carcanet Press (2000); **Kit Wright**, 'The Frozen Man', 'Red Boots On', 'All of Us' and 'The Magic Box', by permission of the author.

Every effort has been made to trace the copyright holders, but if any have been inadvertently overlooked then the publishers will be pleased to make the necessary arrangement at the first opportunity.